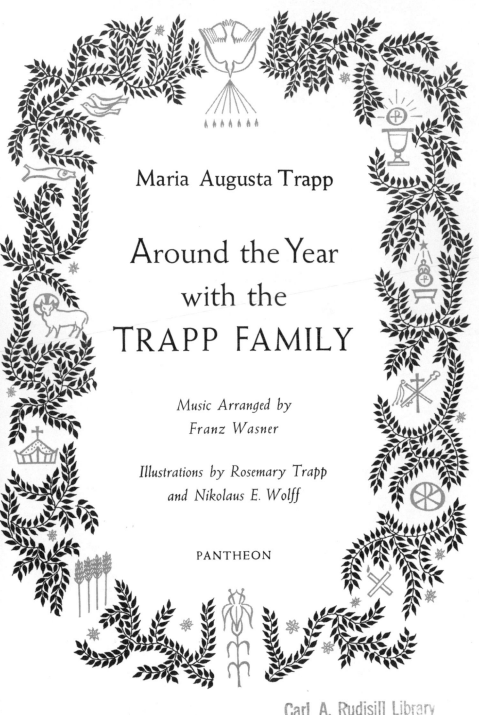

Maria Augusta Trapp

Around the Year
with the
TRAPP FAMILY

Music Arranged by
Franz Wasner

Illustrations by Rosemary Trapp
and Nikolaus E. Wolff

PANTHEON

264.021

T68a

33217

Jan, 1956

The quotations on pp. 35, 36, 106 and 107,
courtesy of Harcourt, Brace & Co., New York.

CONTENTS

LIST OF SONGS

INTRODUCTION

ONCE I watched the transplanting of a full-grown tree. It was a big tree with a wide crown and it had come a far distance. The most amazing thing, however, was that the tree brought an enormous clump of dirt along, almost as big as its crown. The gardener explained to me that grown trees cannot be transplanted as saplings are—the latter are taken out of the soil by the roots and put into their new place without minding it in the least.

"The roots of the grown tree wouldn't take to a new environment, so we have to bring it in its own home-dirt." And the old German gardener used the word *"Heimaterde."*

A year later, on a very hot day, I passed through that town again. I remembered that tree and felt impelled to look it up. When I found it, it looked as if it had always grown there, holding out its wide branches protectingly over a group of people who enjoyed its cool shade.

When a whole family group has to be transplanted from one continent to another, it is very much the same. When Hitler's troops invaded our homeland, Austria, in 1938, my husband and I felt bound in conscience to save our children from yielding to the religion and philosophy of this neo-paganism, and this could only be done by transplanting the whole big tree. The exciting story of this adventure —for every transplanting of a grown tree is an adventure—I have told in my first book, *The Story of the Trapp Family Singers.* Here I only want to write about one aspect of it.

When we finally reached the hospitable shores of this country, we arrived in New York City, the fourteen of us, possessing a total of four dollars. Most of us knew no English and we had no relatives or friends on this vast continent. We were real refugees and we were really poor.

Or so we thought! Soon we were to discover the surprising news that although we had no money, we were not poor at all. The Heavenly Father, Who had done the transplanting, had left all the necessary dirt around the roots. The inner environment of the tree, that part which is hidden from the eye, had not been touched: our family life, as we were used to living it around the year, went on undisturbed as before. Every day found us gathered around the altar in the morning, then trying to find and live the Will of God as it showed itself in each particular day to each one of us until we met again together for evening prayer and blessing; then there would be Sunday, celebrated by manifesting more love of God and love of neighbor; and the weeks would pass, and the rhythm of the year of the Church, with all its moods and rich meanings—the happy expectancy of Advent, the fulfillment of Christmas, the sorrow of Lent and Holy Week, the glory of Easter and Pentecost—would become a powerful force in our daily life. In this "school of living" Holy Mother Church teaches her children how to celebrate. In it one learns how to turn family days such as birthdays, anniversaries, baptisms, weddings, and even funerals into feasts celebrated in the Lord.

Storms, sometimes gale-size, may trouble the crown of the tree, but as long as its roots are firmly imbedded, the healthy tree will weather many a tempest. And not only that! It will share its own well-being with all the ones who need its cool shade for protection from the heat of noon.

More and more often, friends who happened to drop in on our Sundays and feast days would say afterwards: "These lovely old folk customs of yours—couldn't they be introduced in our homes too? They really are not necessarily Austrian or Polish or Italian—they are Catholic, which is universal."

I realize of course that the customs that accompany our life are predominantly Austrian, and that other countries have developed other ways of sanctifying life, equally valid. Still, our Austrian ones are an expression of a deeply Catholic feeling, and they have grown out of times and from people who found it natural to carry over their beliefs into the forms of everyday life. I also realize that traditions cannot be simply imitated. But if some of my readers find in this book hints that will make Catholic home life more warm and expressive of our religion, and above all that will bring children and parents closer together, in adolescence as well as in early youth, I will feel happy in the thought that the tree has been able to thank its new country, by passing on some of the strength it brought here with the earth around its roots.

Celebrating
with the
Family in Heaven

Christmas Season

Advent

THE EVENTS that come to mind when we say "Christmas," "Easter," "Pentecost," are so tremendous that their commemoration cannot be celebrated in a single day each. Weeks are needed. First, weeks of preparation, of becoming attuned in body and soul, and then weeks of celebration. This goes back to an age when people still had time—time to live, time to enjoy. In our own day, we face the puzzling fact that the more time-saving gadgets we invent, the more new buttons to push in order to "save hours of work"—the less time we actually have. We have no more time to read books; we can only afford digests. We have no time to walk a quarter of a mile; we have to hop into a car. We have no time to make things by hand; we buy them ready made in the five-and-ten or in the supermarket. This atmosphere of "hurry up, let's go" does not provide the necessary leisure in which to anticipate and celebrate a feast. But as soon as people stop celebrating they really do not *live* any more—they are *being* lived, as it were. The alarming question arises: what is being done with all the time that is constantly being saved? We invent more machines and more gadgets, which will relieve us more and more from the work formerly done by our hands, our feet, our brain, and which will carry us in feverishly increasing speed—where? Perhaps to the moon and other planets, but more probably to our final destruction.

Only the Church throws light onto the gloomy prospects of modern man—Holy Mother Church—for she belongs, herself, to a realm

14

that has its past and present in Time, but its future in the World Without End.

It was fall when we arrived in the United States. The first weeks passed rapidly, filled with new discoveries every day, and soon we came across a beautiful feast, which we had never celebrated before: Thanksgiving Day, an exclusively American feast. With great enthusiasm we included it in the calendar of our family feasts.

Who can describe our astonishment, however, when a few days after our first Thanksgiving Day we heard from a loudspeaker in a large department store the unmistakable melody of "Silent Night"! Upon our excited inquiry, someone said, rather surprised: "What is the matter? Nothing is the matter. Time for Christmas shopping!"

It took several Christmas seasons before we understood the connection between Christmas shopping and "Silent Night" and the other carols blaring from loudspeakers in these pre-Christmas weeks. And even now that we do understand, it still disturbs us greatly. These weeks before Christmas, known as the weeks of Advent, are meant to be spent in expectation and waiting. This is the season for Advent songs—those age-old hymns of longing and waiting; "Silent Night" should be sung for the first time on Christmas Eve. We found that hardly anybody knows any Advent songs. And we were startled by something else: soon after Christmas, Christmas trees and decorations vanish from the show windows to be replaced by New Year's advertisements. On our concert trips across the country we also saw that the lighted Christmas trees disappear from homes and front yards and no one thinks to sing a carol as late as January 2nd. This was all very strange to us, for we were used to the old-world Christmas, which was altogether different but which we determined to celebrate now in our new country.

THE ADVENT WREATH

In the week before the first Sunday in Advent, we began to inquire where we could obtain the various things necessary to make an Advent wreath.

"A what?" was the invariable answer, accompanied by a blank look.

And we learned that nobody seemed to know what an Advent wreath is. (This was fifteen years ago.) For us it was not a question of whether or not we would have an Advent wreath. The wreath was a must. Advent would be unthinkable without it. The question was only how to get it in a country where nobody seemed to know about it.

Back in Austria we used to go to a toy shop and buy a large hoop, about three feet in diameter. Then we would tie hay around it, three inches thick, as a foundation; and around this we would make a beautiful wreath of balsam twigs. The whole was about three feet in diameter and ten inches thick. As we tried the different toy shops in Philadelphia, the sales people only smiled indulgently and made us feel like Rip Van Winkle. "Around the turn of the century" they had sold the last hoop.

"Necessity is the mother of invention." Martina, who had made the Advent wreath during our last Advents back home, decided to buy strong wire at a hardware store and braid it into a round hoop. Then she tied old newspaper around it, instead of hay, and went out to look for balsam twigs. We lived in Germantown, a suburb of Philadelphia. Martina looked at all the evergreens in our friends' gardens, but there was no balsam fir. So she chose the next best and came home with a laundry basket full of twigs from a yew tree. In the hardware store, where she had bought the wire, she also got four tall spikes, which she worked into her newspaper reel as candle-holders, and in the five-and-ten next door she bought a few yards of strong red ribbon and four candles. The yew twigs made a somewhat feathery Advent wreath; but, said Martina, "It's round and it's made of evergreen, and that is all that is necessary." And she was right. An Advent wreath is round as a symbol of God's mercy of which every season of Advent is a new reminder; and it has to be made of evergreens to symbolize God's "everlastingness."

This was the only Advent we celebrated at home because the manager who arranged the concerts for us had discovered that our tenth child would soon arrive and had cancelled the concerts for the

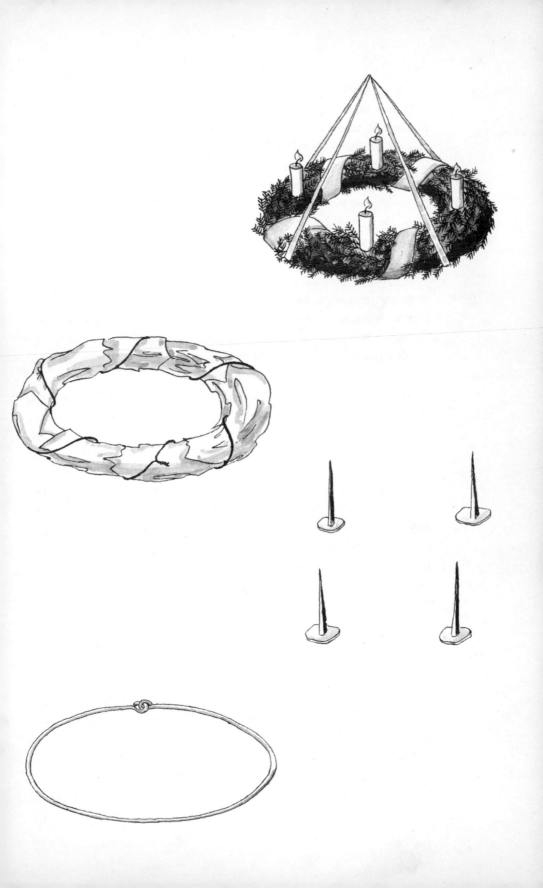

month of December. In the next few years a much smaller Advent
wreath would be made by our children and fastened to the ceiling
of the big blue bus in which we toured the country. We always
started out by looking for balsam fir, but not until years later, when
we were to have our own farm in Vermont, would we have a balsam
Advent wreath again. Meanwhile we had to take what we could find
in the way of evergreens: in Georgia it was holly; in Virginia, box-
wood; in Florida, pine. The least desirable of all was spruce, which
we used the year we travelled through Wisconsin, because spruce
loses its needles quickest. But as long as it was an evergreen. . . .

In order to get ready for the celebration of the beginning of Advent, one more thing has to be added: a tall, thick candle, the Advent
candle, as a symbol of Him Whom we call "the Light of the World."
During these weeks of Advent it will be the only light for the family
evening prayer. Its feeble light is the symbol and reminder of mankind's state of spiritual darkness during Advent.

On the first of January a new calendar year begins. On the first
Sunday of Advent the new year of the Church begins. Therefore,
the Saturday preceding the first Advent Sunday has something of
the character of a New Year's Eve. One of the old customs is to
choose a patron saint for the new year of the Church. The family
meets on Saturday evening, and with the help of the missal and a
book called *The Martyrology*, which lists thousands of saints as
they are celebrated throughout the year, they choose as many new
saints as there are members of the household. We always choose
them according to a special theme. One year, for instance, we had all
the different Church Fathers; another year we chose only martyrs;
then again, only saints of the new world. . . . During the war we
chose one saint of every country at war.

The newly chosen names are handed over to the calligrapher of
the family (first it was Johanna; after she married, Rosemary took
over). She writes the names of the saints in gothic lettering on little
cards. Then she writes the name of every member of the household
on an individual card and hands the two sets over to the mother.
Now everything is ready.

In the afternoon of the first Sunday of Advent, around vesper time, the whole family—and this always means "family" in the larger sense of the word, including all the members of the household—meets in the living room. The Advent wreath hangs suspended from the ceiling on four red ribbons; the Advent candle stands in the middle of the table or on a little stand on the side. Solemnly the father lights one candle on the Advent wreath, and, for the first time, the big Advent candle. Then he reads the Gospel of the first Sunday of Advent. After this the special song of Advent is intoned for the first time, the ancient "Ye heavens, dew drop from above, and rain ye clouds the Just One. . . ."

It cannot be said often enough that during these weeks before Christmas, songs and hymns of Advent should be sung. No Christmas carols! Consciously we should work toward restoring the true character of waiting and longing to these precious weeks before Christmas. Just before Midnight Mass, on December 24th, is the moment to sing for the first time "Silent Night, Holy Night," for this is the song for this very night. It may be repeated afterwards as many times as we please, but it should not be sung before that holy night.

Since we have found that Advent hymns have been largely forgotten, we want to include here the ones we most often sing; and we also want to explain how we collected our songs. First, there were a certain number, the traditional ones, which were still sung in homes and in church during the weeks of Advent. Then we looked for collections in libraries; we inquired among friends and acquaintances; we wrote to people we had met on our travels in foreign countries. Each song that has come to us in this way is particularly dear to us—a personal friend rather than a chance acquaintance.

YOU HEAVENS, DEW DROP FROM ABOVE

Text, Isaias 45,8; melody, first (Dorian) mode. This is the medieval Advent call—sing three times, each time a tone higher.

O COME, O COME, EMMANUEL

The text of this hymn is based on the seven Great Antiphons (O-Antiphons) which are said before and after the Magnificat at Vespers from December 17 to 23. The metrical Latin form dates from the early 18th century. English translation J. M. Neale (1818-1866), and *The Hymnal of the Protestant Episcopal Church in U.S.A.* (stanzas 2 and 4), by permission of The Church Pension Fund. Melody, first (Dorian) mode.

ex - ile here Un-til the Son of God ap-pear
Em-ma - nu - el

Re-joice! Re-joice! Em-ma - nu - -el

Is - ra - el.

Shall come to thee, O Is - ra - el!

2. O come, Thou Wisdom from on high,
   Who ordrest all things mightily;
   To us the path of knowledge show,
   And teach us in her ways to go.—Refrain

3. O come, Thou Key of David, come,
   And open wide our heav'nly home;
   Make safe the way that leads to thee,
   And close the path to misery.—Refrain

4. O come, Desire of Nations, bind
   In one the hearts of all mankind;
   Bid Thou our sad divisions cease,
   And be thyself our King of Peace.—Refrain

DROP YOUR DEW, YE CLOUDS OF HEAVEN

Text, Michael Denis, 1774; melody, 18th century Austrian,
probably Michael Haydn, 1737-1806.

Drop your dew, ye clouds of heav-en, Rain the Just One now to save! With that cry the night was riv - en From the world, a yawning grave. On the earth by God for- sak- en Sin and death their toll had tak- en. Tightly

shut was heaven's gate, For sal - va - tion all must wait.

2. To redeem our sad condition
   Was the Father's loving Will,
   And the Son took the glad mission
   His decision to fulfill.
   Gabriel to earth descended,
   Brought the answer long attended:
   "See the Handmaid of the Lord,
   Do according to thy word."

3. Let us walk with right intention,
   Not in drunkenness and greed,
   Quarrels, envies and contention
   Banished far from us indeed.
   Fully now to imitate Him
   As with longing we await Him
   Is the duty of these days,
   As the great Apostle says.

O SAVIOUR, HEAVEN'S PORTAL REND

Text and melody, 17th century German. This forceful melody
in the first (Dorian) mode should be sung in unison.

O Sav - iour, heav - en's por- tals rend;

Come down, from heav'n, to earth de - scend!

O - pen ce - les - tial gate and door;

Nev- er to lock nor fast - en more.

2. O brilliant Sun, O lovely Star,
   We dare behold Thee from afar.
   O Sun arise; without Thy light
   We languish all in darkest night.

3. Drop dew, ye heavens from above,
   Come in the dew, O God of love!
   Ye clouds now break, rain down the King,
   His peace to Jacob's house to bring.

MARIA WALKS AMID THE THORN

German folksong known since the 16th century; probably much older. Translation, Henry S. Drinker.

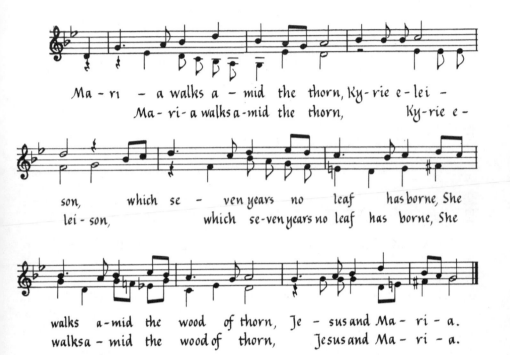

Ma - ri - a walks a - mid the thorn, Ky-rie e-lei -
Ma - ri - a walks a-mid the thorn, Ky-rie e -

son, which se - ven years no leaf has borne, She
lei - son, which se-ven years no leaf has borne, She

walks a-mid the wood of thorn, Je - sus and Ma - ri - a.
walks a - mid the wood of thorn, Jesus and Ma - ri - a.

2. *What 'neath her heart does Mary bear?*
Kyrie eleison.
A little child does Mary bear,
Beneath her heart He nestles there.
Jesus and Maria.

3. *And as the two are passing near,*
Kyrie eleison,
Lo! roses on the thorns appear,
Lo! roses on the thorns appear.
Jesus and Maria.

BLESSED MOTHER OF THE SAVIOUR

Text by Hermann the Cripple, 1013-1054, monk at Reichenau in the Lake of Constance. Melody in the fifth (Lydian) mode. This is the liturgical Antiphon in honor of the Blessed Virgin for the season of Advent and Christmas.

Bles — sed Mo-ther of the Sav-ior, thou art the gate lead-ing us to heav-en, and Star of the Sea, aid thy fal-ling peo-ple, help all those who seek to rise a-gain. Thou who art the Mo-ther, all na-ture won-der-ing, to thy Lord, thy own Cre-a-tor: Vir-gin be-fore, Vir-gin for-ev-er, from Ga-bri-el's mouth thou didst hear that bles-sed A-ve, on us poor sin-ners take pi-ty.

After our first gathering around the Advent light, and the singing of the first Advent hymn, an air of expectancy spreads over the family group; now comes the moment when the mother goes around with a bowl in which are the little cards with the names of the new saints. Everybody draws a card and puts it in his missal. This saint will be invoked every morning after morning prayer. Everyone is supposed to look up and study the life story of his new friend, and some time during the coming year he will tell the family all about it. As there are so many of us, we come to know about different saints every year. Sometimes this calls for considerable research on the part of the unfortunate one who has drawn St. Eustachius, for instance, or St. Bibiana. But the custom has become very dear to us, and every year it seems as if the family circle were enlarged by all those new brothers and sisters entering in and becoming known and loved by all.

And then comes another exciting moment. Once more the mother appears with the bowl, which she passes around. This time the pieces of paper contain the names of the members of the family and are neatly rolled up, because the drawing has to be done in great secrecy. The person whose name one has drawn is now in one's special care. From this day until Christmas, one has to do as many little favors for him or her as one can. One has to provide at least one surprise every single day—but without ever being found out. This creates a wonderful atmosphere of joyful suspense, kindness, and thoughtfulness. Perhaps you will find that somebody has made your bed or shined your shoes or has informed you, in a disguised handwriting on a holy card, that "a rosary has been said for you today" or a number of sacrifices have been offered up. This new relationship is called "*Christkindl*" (Christ Child) in the old country, where children believe that the Christmas tree and the gifts under it are brought down by the Christ Child himself.

The beautiful thing about this particular custom is that the relationship is a reciprocal one. The person whose name I have drawn and who is under my care becomes for me the helpless little Christ Child in the manger; and as I am performing these many little acts of love and consideration for someone in the family I am really doing them for the Infant of Bethlehem, according to the word, "And he that shall receive one such little child in my name, receiveth me." That is why this particular person turns into "my *Christkindl.*" At the same time I am the *Christkindl* also for the one I am caring for because I want to imitate the Holy Child and render all those little services in the same spirit as He did in that small house of Nazareth, when as a child He served His Mother and His foster father with a similar love and devotion.

Many times throughout these weeks can be heard such exclamations as, "I have a wonderful *Christkindl* this year!" or, "Goodness, I forgot to do something for my *Christkindl* and it is already suppertime!" It is a delightful custom, which creates much of the true Christmas spirit and ought to be spread far and wide.

And there is still one very important thing to do for Advent. According to Austrian custom, every member of the family writes a letter to the Holy Child mentioning his resolutions for the weeks of Advent and listing all his wishes for gifts. This *"Christkindl Brief"* (letter to the Holy Child) is put on the window sill, from whence the Guardian Angel will take it up to heaven to read it aloud to the Holy Child.

To make small children (and older ones, too) aware of the happy expectancy of Advent, there is a special Advent calendar which clever hands can make at home. It might be a house with windows for each day of Advent; every morning the child opens another window, behind which appears a star, an angel, or some other picture appropriate to the season. On the 23rd, all windows are open, but the big entrance door still is closed. That is opened on Christmas Eve, when it reveals the Holy Child in the manger, or a Christmas tree. All kinds of variations on this theme are possible, such as the Jacob's Ladder shown on our illustration, which leads step by step to the day of Christ's birth. All such little aids make Christmas more wonderful and "special" to a child, and preparing them adds to our own Christmas joy.

Advent Calendar: Take piece of cardboard; cut out clouds, leaving them attached at one point so that they can fold out. Cut spaces in ladder as on insert so that they can fold down. Take transparent paper same size as cardboard. Paint and draw pictures of stars, angels, toys, etc. on spots behind clouds and ladder steps. For top cloud, put Christmas tree or Christ Child in crib. Paste this on back of calendar. Each day another cloud or ladder step should be opened, until Christmas Eve is reached on top of ladder.

ST. BARBARA'S DAY

There is a group of fourteen saints known as the "Fourteen Auxiliary Saints." In Austria they are sometimes pictured together in an old chapel, or over a side altar of a church; each one has an attribute by which he may be recognized—St. George will be shown with a dragon, or St. Blaise with two candles crossed. One of these Auxiliary Saints is St. Barbara, whose feast is celebrated on December 4th. She can be recognized by her tower (in which she was kept prisoner) and the ciborium surmounted by the Sacred Host. St. Barbara is invoked against lightning and sudden death. She is the patron saint of miners and artillery men and she is also invoked by young unmarried girls to pick the right husband for them.

On the fourth of December, unmarried members of the household are supposed to go out into the orchard and cut twigs from the cherry trees and put them into water. There is an old belief that whoever's cherry twig blossoms on Christmas Day can expect to get married in the following year. As most of us are always on tour at this time of the year, someone at home will be commissioned to "cut the cherry twigs." These will be put in a vase in a dark corner, each one with a name tag, and on Christmas Day they will be eagerly examined; and even if they are good for nothing else, they provide a nice table decoration for the Christmas dinner.

ST. NICHOLAS' DAY

Although St. Nicholas is not in the illustrious company of the Fourteen Auxiliary Saints, he has been one of the most popular saints in the East and in the West for many hundreds of years. He is the patron of seafarers and also of scholars, bankers, and—thieves. But most of all, he is the very special saint of children. Devotion to St. Nicholas is found in every European country. In the north, in Scandinavia and in northern Germany, he is known as Santa Claus. I do not know what happened to him on his way from Europe to America. While he is still pictured in the old world as an ascetic-looking bishop with cope, mitre, and crozier, since crossing the ocean he has turned into a fat, jolly, red-nosed, elderly gentleman in a snowsuit and a red cap. From Lapland he has brought his reindeer. Unfortunately, he has changed the date of his appearance. In the old country he comes on the evening before his feast day (the feast of St. Nicholas, on December 6th), accompanied by the *"Krampus,"* an ugly, chain-rattling little devil, who has to deal with the children who have been naughty. St. Nicholas is much too kind to do the punishing and scolding himself.

It all goes back to the days when St. Nicholas was Bishop of Myra, where he once discreetly threw alms in through a window as a dowry for three young girls, who would otherwise have been sold into slavery, according to the custom of the day. For this good deed God rewarded him by giving him permission to walk the streets of earth on the eve of his feast, bringing gifts to all good children.

While in some places the children only put their shoes on the window sill on the eve of St. Nicholas' Day and find them filled with candies, cookies, oranges, and dried fruit the next morning (but only the good ones; the bad ones find a switch), in other parts St. Nicholas comes in person. He always did in our house. On the eve of December 5th the whole family would gather in the living room with great expectancy. By the time the much-expected knock at the door could be heard, one could almost hear the anxious heartbeat of the little ones. The holy bishop, in his pontifical vestments, accompanied by Krampus, would enter the room while everybody stood up reverently. St. Nicholas always carried a thick book in which the Guardian Angels make their entries throughout the year. That's why the saint has such an an astonishing knowledge about everybody. He calls each member of the household forward, rewarding the good and admonishing the less good. The good children will get a package of sweets, whereas Krampus aims at the legs of the children who did not deserve one. After everyone has received his due, the holy bishop addresses a few words of general admonition to the whole family, acting as a precursor to the One Who is to come, drawing their thoughts toward Christmas, asking them to prepare their hearts for the coming of the Holy Child. After giving his blessing, he takes his leave, accompanied reverently by the mother, who opens the door for him. Soon afterwards the father, who, oddly enough, usually misses this august visit, will come home, and he has to hear everything about it from the youngest in the house.

Of course it did not occur to us, even in the first and second years in America, that St. Nicholas' Day should pass without the dear saint's appearing in our family circle. In the old home this beloved bishop's attire was stored away in the attic to be used every year on the evening before his feast, but now we had to work with cardboard and paper for the mitre, a bed sheet for an alb, a golden damask curtain borrowed from friends for a cope, and a broomstick artistically transformed into a bishop's staff. But at the right moment St. Nicholas opened the door. That taught us that it really does not require money, but only imagination and good will, to revive or introduce these lovely old customs.

"St. Nicholas smells of Christmas, don't you think, Mother?" one of my little girls said once, meaning that on December 5th the whole house was filled with the same good smell as it would be in the days just before Christmas. For this day there is a special kind of cookie called *Speculatius.* The dough is rolled very thin and then cut in the shape of St. Nicholas, and these little figures are then decorated with icing in different colors and candied fruit. And just as we are sharing with the reader our ancient songs and customs, I believe we should also share those ancient recipes that have come down to us through the centuries. So here is the recipe for *Speculatius* (St. Nicholas). It comes from Holland.

Speculatius

1 cup butter	4 tsp. cinnamon
1 cup lard	½ tsp. nutmeg
2 cups brown sugar	½ tsp. cloves
½ cup sour cream	4½ cups sifted flour
½ tsp. soda	½ cup chopped nuts

Cream the butter, lard, and sugar. Add sour cream alternately with sifted dry ingredients. Stir in nuts. Knead the dough into rolls. Wrap the rolls in waxed paper and chill in the refrigerator overnight. Roll the dough very thin and cut it into shapes. Bake in moderate oven 10 to 15 minutes.

Another family recipe must not be forgotten here. As we are a rather cosmopolitan family, with one branch of English relatives and with my husband's people coming from northern Germany, and sprinkled with cousins from France and Italy and Switzerland, not to mention personal culinary memories of my husband's early years in the Balkans and our own far-flung journeys, we have quite a number of recipes. This one is a venerated old "must"—a real British plum pudding. It has to be started on the first Sunday of Advent, which in England is still known to this day as "Stir-Up Sunday." There is an old belief that the more you stir a pudding the better it will be, and that each member of the household must come for a good stir. Plum pudding is painstaking to make, and time-consuming, but when it finally appears on the table, aflame with burning brandy, everyone agrees that it was worth the trouble and it wouldn't be Christmas without it.

Plum Pudding

1 lb. suet	1 fresh orange peel
3 cups brown sugar	¼ lb. candied orange peel
2 cups stale breadcrumbs	¼ lb. candied grapefruit peel
6 eggs	1½ lb. raisins
juice of ten oranges	½ lb. currants
4 cups sifted flour	½ lb. citron
1 tsp. ginger	¼ lb. blanched almonds
1 tsp. salt	2 medium-size raw potatoes
1 tsp. cinnamon	2 medium-size raw apples
1 tsp. nutmeg	2 medium-size raw carrots
1 fresh lemon peel	

Grind the suet and bread. Moisten with beaten eggs and orange juice. Add sifted dry ingredients. Grind fresh and candied peel with the raw vegetables. Add these to the batter. Stir in raisins, currants, citron, and almonds. If the pudding is dry or lumpy, add fruit juice. Pack in buttered tins and steam.

"And steam" is taken literally in our house, even now in the days of the pressure cooker. It takes a whole day, eight to ten hours, but then the pudding keeps indefinitely, or, rather, it improves with time.

As I write this we have just begun the holy season of Advent.

Yesterday there was in my mail a somewhat bulky, large envelope and when I picked it up, something rattled. I found a Christmas card from our good friends the Sisters of Social Service, and a little brown envelope containing seeds (that, of course, explained the rattling). "Christmas wheat," it said. When I read the explanation, I was happy to know that here was a group who wanted to share a folk custom from their old home—the Sisters of Social Service were founded in Hungary—with their friends in America. With the permission of the Sisters, I pass on the story of this lovely custom, feeling sure that many of us will wish to adopt it.

THE MEANING OF THE CHRISTMAS WHEAT

It is an ancient Hungarian custom to offer to the Infant in the manger the green sprouts of wheat.

Agriculture is the mainstay of the Hungarian nation and wheat is the symbol of sustenance and prosperity for this nation. It is therefore the most suitable gift for the newborn Saviour.

But it also has a meaning for everyone. The "new wheat" symbolizes the "new bread" in the natural order and also the "New Bread of Life" in the supernatural order; for it is from wheat that the altar bread is made which becomes the Holy Eucharist, the bread of our souls.

The wheat seeds are planted on the day of St. Lucy, the virgin martyr, December 13th. Kept in a moderately warm room and watered daily, the plant reaches its full growth by Christmas. The little daily care given to it is flavored with the joy of expectation for the approaching Christmas and spreads the spirit of cheerfulness as the tender plant reminds us of our spiritual rebirth through the mysteries of Christmas.

To plant the seeds, take a flower pot four or five inches in height and fill it with plain garden sod. Spread the seeds on the top and press gently, so that the seeds are covered with sod. Do not push them too deep.

Watered daily at the manger and paying its simple homage to the newborn Saviour, the plant will last until about January 6th.

"O all ye things that spring up in the earth, bless the Lord."
(*Canticle of the Three Children*)

THE CHRISTMAS CRIB

If asked about the origin of these old folk customs, one sometimes finds it hard to answer. They have come down to us through the centuries out of the gray past. Some are so old that they go back to pre-Christian times, having been baptized together with the people and turned from pagan into Christian customs. But once in a while we know how one or the other custom originated. The Christmas crib as we have it today goes back to St. Francis of Assisi. Not that he was the one who made the first crèche. This devotion is almost as old as the Church. We are told that the very place of Christ's birth and the manger in which He lay "wrapped in swaddling clothes" were already venerated in Bethlehem in the first centuries of the Christian era. Later devout people substituted a silver manger for the original one and built a basilica over it; and, with the centuries, the veneration of the Holy Child lying in the manger spread all over the Christian countries. More and more ceremonies sprang up around this devotion, until in medieval times they had grown into a real theatre performance—drama, opera, and ballet combined. Finally, Pope Honorius had to put a stop to this, for it had grown into an abuse. A generation later St. Francis of Assisi got permission for his famous Christmas celebration in the woods of Greccio near Assisi, on Christmas Eve, 1223. His first biographer, Thomas of Celano, tells us how it happened:

> It should be recorded and held in reverent memory what Blessed Francis did near the town of Greccio, on the feast day of the Nativity of our Lord Jesus Christ, three years before his glorious death. In that town lived a certain man by the name of John (Messer Giovanni Velitta) who stood in high esteem, and whose life was even better than his reputation. Blessed Francis loved him with a special affection because, being very noble and much honored, he despised the nobility of the flesh and strove after the nobility of the soul.
>
> Blessed Francis often saw this man. He now called him about two weeks before Christmas and said to him: "If you desire that we

should celebrate this year's Christmas together at Greccio, go quickly and prepare what I tell you; for I want to enact the memory of the Infant who was born at Bethlehem and how He was deprived of all the comforts babies enjoy; how He was bedded in the manger on hay between an ass and an ox. For once I want to see all this with my own eyes." When that good and faithful man had heard this, he departed quickly and prepared in the above-mentioned place everything that the Saint had told him.

The joyful day approached. The Brethren [the Friars who had gathered around St. Francis] were called from many communities. The men and women of the neighborhood, as best they could, prepared candles and torches to brighten the night. Finally the Saint of God arrived, found everything prepared, saw it and rejoiced. The crib was made ready, hay was brought, the ox and ass were led to the spot. . . . Greccio became a new Bethlehem. The night was made radiant like the day, filling men and animals with joy. The crowds drew near and rejoiced in the novelty of the celebration. Their voices resounded from the woods, and the rocky cliffs echoed the jubilant outburst. As they sang in praise of God the whole night rang with exultation. The Saint of God stood before the crib, overcome with devotion and wondrous joy. A solemn Mass was sung at the crib.

The Saint, dressed in deacon's vestments, for a deacon he was, sang the Gospel. Then he preached a delightful sermon to the people who stood around him, speaking about the nativity of the poor King and the humble town of Bethlehem. . . . And whenever he mentioned the Child of Bethlehem or the Name of Jesus, he seemed to lick his lips as if he would happily taste and swallow the sweetness of that word.*

That is the beginning of the crèche as we know it in our own day. St. Francis' idea of bringing Bethlehem into one's own town spread quickly all over the Christian world, and when there was a Christmas crib in every church, the families began to re-enact the birth of Christ in their homes too. With loving imagination, more or less elaborately, the little town of Bethlehem would be reconstructed. There would be the cave with the manger, "because there was no room at the inn," and the figures would be carved in wood

* Celano, "Life and Miracles of St. Francis," as quoted in Francis X. Weiser, *The Christmas Book*, pp. 106 f., New York, Harcourt, Brace & Co.

or modelled in clay or worked after the fashion of puppets. They also might be drawn and painted and then glued on wood.

In some countries whole valleys would take up the carving of these figures—as in Tyrolia and southern Bavaria. Some of these crèches are works of great art. On the long winter evenings, during the weeks of Advent, the people are working on them. First, the scenery is set up again, and then the figures are placed, each year seeing some new additions, until such a crib fills almost a whole room with its hundreds of figures.

Outside the town of Bethlehem, Connecticut, the nuns of the Benedictine Priory, "Regina Laudis," have devoted a whole building to their huge Christmas crib, a Neapolitan work that was given to them as a gift. This beautiful crib could become an American shrine, the center for a pilgrimage during the Christmas season.

Just as the Reformation did away with statues and pictures of saints in Protestant churches, it also deprived many Protestant homes of the crèche. A few of the German sects, however, kept up this custom even after the Reformation, and brought it to America. When the Moravians, for example, founded the town of Bethlehem, Pennsylvania, on a Christmas Eve, they had preserved the custom of the crèche.

At home in Austria we wanted a crèche which we could make mostly by ourselves. That is why we did not buy one of the ready-made models, but went out into the woods with the children before the first snowfall and carried home stones, moss, bark, lichen, and pine cones. A large table-top, three by five feet, was placed over two carpenter's sawhorses and draped with green cloth. This was the foundation on which every year a slightly different scene would be erected by artistic young hands—the stony hill with the cave, the field, covered with moss, with shepherds in the foreground. For the figures we bought only the heads and hands, beautifully modelled in wax at a little store in Salzburg that sold handmade and artistically decorated candles and *Lebkuchen*. At home we made the foundation of the figures with wire and then dressed them with loving care, and it is incredible what ingenious hands can produce with a needle and thread and remnants of dress material. Every evening

Top left: How to make the manger. Cut heavy paper to size, fold along dotted lines and glue together; cut other pieces from wood and mount together as in right picture.

Center left: Cut enough strips of paper and fold into round sleeves to fit over wire stem of palm on right; do not attach top wires until stem is covered; make crown of palm from wire and tie on stem; cut leaves from folded green paper as shown in drawing; cut fringes; unfold slightly and mount on branches of palm tree. See final palm in crib scene.

Bottom: Model wire puppet for crib figures.

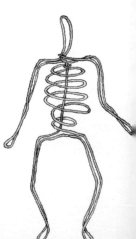

GLORIA IN EXCELSIS DEO

Cut figurine heads from blocks of plaster of Paris or mold them in wax. Dress them with cloth.

Cut sheep from plaster of Paris or wood, paint them.

Cave: Use cardboard to get general shape and build around with stone and moss. Carve animals same way as sheep.

Angel: Make same way as other figures, attach cardboard wings on which you glue gold foil. Make streamer from light board. Stitch on to hands of angel.

during Advent some time was devoted to the crèche. At the end of the first week the landscape was completed; the second week was animal week, at the end of which many little sheep were grazing on the meadow and the ox was standing in the cave. In the third week the shepherds appeared, watching their sheep in little groups; while in the fourth week Mary and Joseph could be seen approaching from afar with the little ass, advancing steadily every day. Finally, on Christmas Eve, they reached the cave. The ass joined the ox behind the empty manger. Mary was kneeling down in expectation (that's the beauty of the wire under the blue dress: the figures can kneel, stand, or sit), while Saint Joseph hung up a lantern above the manger and everyone seemed to hold his breath, waiting until just before Midnight Mass. Then the youngest member of the family would put the little Baby into the manger and joy would reach its height. After Midnight Mass, the figure of the big angel would appear, suspended on a long wire above the shepherds, announcing, "Glory to God in the Highest." There is no telling how much love and joy goes into the making of such a crib year after year.

Again I must go back to our first year in this country. Of course, Christmas without a crib under the tree would for us have been Christmas with something essential missing. The beloved figures of our Christmas crib, however, were among the things we had left behind. But now the older children's Christmas present to me in that memorable first year turned out to be a large, elaborate Christmas crib with the figures and the little town of Bethlehem, self-designed, cut out of cardboard and hand-painted. Our neighbors in Germantown had kindly invited the children to help themselves in their gardens to the necessary bark, moss, and stones.

In addition to the large Christmas crib in the living room, we had one more custom in our family as long as the children were little. We used to place in the nursery a large wooden crib which could hold an almost life-size Infant Jesus. On the first Sunday in Advent it would be empty, but a big bag full of straw would rest beside it. Every evening, after the family evening prayers, each child could take as many pieces of straw from the bag as it had performed sacrifices and good deeds during the day "in order to please the Infant

Jesus"—in other words, out of love of God. This is a precious opportunity for a mother to teach her little ones the true nature of a sacrifice brought voluntarily for the love of God. Meal times furnish
excellent occasions for self-denial. To take an extra helping of an
unpopular vegetable or to pass up a delicious dessert may be a real
sacrifice for a child. So Hedwig ate a whole plateful of very healthy
but unloved beets, while Martina followed the chocolate cake with
longing eyes, saying, "No, thank you," however. Toys gave another
opportunity for self-denial. I could hardly believe my eyes when I
found Hedwig's favorite doll, "Happy," in Martina's lap, and Martina's little family of dwarfs—Father Dwarf, Mother Dwarf, and
Baby Dwarf—in Johanna's corner, while Johanna had put her otherwise jealously guarded doll house into the middle of the room for
everybody to use. These may be acts of heroism; we have only to
think of the parable of the widow's mite—in the eyes of God she
had given more than any other, for the others gave from their abun-
dance, while she had given all she had.

What a race among the youngsters from evening to evening until
the crib was finally filled to the brim! When, on Christmas Eve, little
Martina—for a long time the youngest among the children—was
allowed to put the Holy Child on His bed of straw, the Infant seemed
to smile at the children, grateful for the soft bed prepared with so
much love. It is curious how such a childhood habit stays with you
through life. You may be grown up, even white-haired, but all during
Advent you will feel the same urge to "collect more straws for the
crib."

SEEKING SHELTER

In the old country we had in our house an oil painting showing St.
Joseph leading the Blessed Mother, who was with Child and looked
fatigued and tired, as they were asking shelter at the inn. Through
the crack of the door one could see the ugly, rough face of the inn-
keeper, and it was rather easy to guess what he had just said. This
picture played a big role during the last part of Advent in the custom
called *Herbergsuchen* (seeking shelter). By lot, nine members of

the household were chosen to be host to this holy couple, to make up for the hard words, each one in turn offering room and shelter for one day. The children, especially, vied with each other, decorating little altars with candles and fir branches and trying to outdo each other in loving care for the august visitors. The one who was the host for the day could have the picture in his room and spend as much time with his holy guests as he wanted and school permitted. He could, for instance, take his meals together with them upstairs. How inspiring this is for the imagination of the very young—sharing even their meals with the poor Holy Mother, who "doesn't look so tired any more and seems to like it here." Every night, before evening prayers, the whole family would gather outside the room where the picture had stayed for the day, and in solemn procession it would be carried through the house accompanied by the singing of Advent songs, until it reached the next resting place. Each evening there would be enacted the scene before the closed door of the inn. We used to sing the old Austrian *Herbergsucherlied*, the song called *"Wer klopfet an"*:

> *Who's knocking at my door?*
>
> *Two people poor and low.*
>
> *What are you asking for?*
>
> *That you may mercy show.*
> *We are, O Sir, in sorry plight,*
> *O grant us shelter here tonight.*

You ask in vain.

We beg a place to rest.

It's "no" again!

You will be greatly blessed.

I told you no!
You cannot stay.
Get out of here and go your way.

When we were in Mexico, we learned that there they have a similar custom, called the Posada. On the nine evenings before Christmas they play the *Herbergsuchen* from house to house. They invite the local priest, who joins the procession, saying prayers. Eight nights the holy couple is refused shelter and on the ninth evening, Christmas Eve, they are let into a house where everything is prepared most lovingly—a large cradle is waiting, and while a statue of the Infant is put on the straw, the cradle is being rocked and a famous lullaby is being chanted, *"A la Rurruru."*

As the weeks of Advent are now our busiest concert season, we have had to give up this custom of *Herbergsuchen*—but only in one way. Every evening of these holy weeks of Advent we sing our Christmas program in a different town. While doing so, we hope we may prepare a warm place for the homeless holy couple in many hearts among our audiences.

CHRISTMAS GIFTS

In ancient Rome, people used to exchange gifts on New Year's Day. According to their means, these might be jewelry, pieces of gold and silver, or just home-made pastry, cookies, and candies. But they were a means of saying "Happy New Year." (In French Canada this custom has been preserved to the present day.)

This is one of the instances where Holy Mother Church took an already existing custom and "baptized" it. When the Apostles brought the Gospel to Rome, the people learned of the Three Wise Men who came from the Orient to present gifts to the newborn King of the Jews. From then on, the old custom was only slightly changed. The exchanging of presents remained, but now it was done in imitation of the Three Holy Kings.

It should be understood that everyone in the family has a present for everybody else; these presents should be precious, though not in terms of money, as they should not be bought, but home-made. This is quite a task in a large family, but fingers become skilled in handicrafts of many kinds: block prints, wood carvings, leather work, needle work, lettering with beautiful illuminations, and clay work. All these, and one's imagination, are called upon to create many beautiful, useful things, which could not be bought for money because they are made not only with the hands but also with the heart.

But it is not of the immediate family alone that we have to think when we make gifts. The true Christmas spirit results in a desire, if only it were possible, to extinguish all suffering, all hunger and need of any kind, all over the world. Inspired by this desire, everyone prepares for some poor or unfortunate member of the community some real substantial Christmas joy. The parcels that have to go a long distance, or even overseas, are made in the first week of Advent, and the boxes are lined with fir branches from our own woods. *"Geben ist seliger als nehmen"* ("To give is more blessed than to receive"), says an old proverb, and these are the weeks of the year to prove how true it is. The very essence of Christmas is to give, give, give—since at the very first Christmas the Heavenly Father gave His only begotten Son to us.

THE OCTAVE OF CHRISTMAS

The great feasts of the Church—Christmas, Easter, Pentecost, Epiphany—are privileged to have an octave. That means that the feast is not over at the end of the first evening, but is celebrated for a whole week. Octaves follow the feast like the train on a beautiful wedding dress. Christmas alone is also *preceded* by an octave. By the seventeenth of December, a week before the great day, not only the children are impatient: the Church herself has become so eager for Christmas that she makes an impassioned appeal to the Messias to come, and to come quickly. From that day on, in the so-called Greater Antiphons at Vespers (from the initial letters they are called the "O-Antiphons") prayer and expectation rise in an ever-growing crescendo. The whole of Advent is characterized by the boundless desire for the coming of Christ expressed in the liturgy, and one can almost feel the increasing impatience in the antiphons for Vespers of the several Sundays: "The Lord comes from afar" (first Sunday); "the Lord will come" (second and third Sundays); "the Lord is near" (fourth Sunday). Throughout the whole season there is a growing emphasis on the Lord's coming—our remembrance of His first coming, our glowing desire for His second coming at this present Christmas, and our great expectation of His final coming in the latter days.

These days of holy impatience should be marked also in the family. The "O-Antiphons" might be written out on a piece of white cardboard, and each day for the main family meal they might be put in the center of the table, and afterwards added to the family's evening prayer.

An old custom comes down from the monasteries of medieval times, where the monks used to get extra treats during this octave before Christmas. For example, on December 19th, when the Church calls on Christ, *"O Radix Jesse"* ("O Root of Jesse"), Brother Gardener brought his choicest vegetables and fruits, with specially beautiful roots among them; or on December 20th, when the Antiphon says, "O Key of David. . . ." Brother Cellarer used his key for the wine cellar and brought out the best wine. Finally, on December 23rd, it was the turn of the Abbot, who came with special gifts to the brothers. This beautiful custom could be restored in families, the members of the house taking turns in providing a surprise at the evening meal, leaving the last day for the father, the day before that for the mother, the day before that for the oldest child, and so on.

There is also the tradition, going back to Honorius of Autun, that connects the "O-Antiphons" with the seven Gifts of the Holy Ghost with which the Holy Child was filled at the moment of His birth.

ST. THOMAS' DAY

Finally, St. Thomas' Day, December 21st, arrives. Throughout the Austrian Alps this is the day when the *Kletzenbrot* has to be baked. *Kletzen* is the Tyrolean word for dried pears, but this bread contains a mixture of dried fruit. There will be one large loaf made for the family breakfast on Christmas morning, and an individual small loaf for every member of the household. This *Kletzenbrot* keeps forever, and it is as wholesome as it is delicious. Try it!

Kletzenbrot

2 cups whole wheat flour
1 cup white flour
⅔ cup brown sugar
3 tsp. baking powder
2 tsp. baking soda
¼ tsp. salt
2 cups buttermilk

1 cup chopped nuts
1 cup chopped prunes
1 cup chopped figs
1 cup chopped dates
½ cup raisins
½ cup currants

Mix sifted dry ingredients in a bowl. Add buttermilk slowly and stir to a smooth dough. Mix in the nuts, raisins, and the rest. Bake in a hot oven for about an hour.

But not only *Kletzenbrot* is being baked—on St. Thomas' Day Christmas baking begins, and from now on the house will be filled with a cloud of delicious smells. Some of this Christmas baking—the choicest delicacies in the realm of cookies and candies—will be hung on the Christmas tree, which is altogether different from an American one. Of the many varieties we always preferred the cookies known as *Lebkuchen* (or *Lebzelten*).* They get better with age, and they are responsible for the unique scent known in our family as "Christmas smell."

Recipes for the various cookies are often jealously guarded in individual families, each one having its own tradition. From the dozens

* *Lebkuchen* means "bread of life," and the name seems to be more than a coincidence when one thinks of it as the traditional bread baked for the birthday of the One Who said, "I have come that you may have life and that you may have it more abundantly." To Austrians, there are some cookies so connected with Christmas that they are an absolute "must." Of these, *Lebkuchen* is Number One.

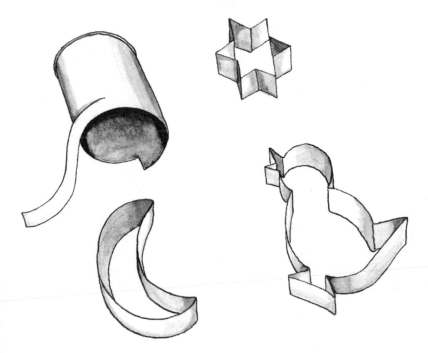

Cookie cutters: Use sturdy shears and cut one inch strips from tin cans; bend into shapes as indicated and fold over joints or solder.

and dozens of delicacies, I shall choose those we consider the eight best, in honor of the eight days of the octave of Christmas—one for each day.

Lebkuchen

4 eggs, beaten
¾ lb. almonds, ground
1 tsp. cinnamon
½ tsp. cloves
⅓ oz. powdered carbonate of potassium

1 lb. sugar
⅛ to ¼ lb. citron
½ lb. honey
3 tbsp. rum or wine
1½ lbs. flour, scant

Dissolve powdered carbonate of potassium in the rum or wine. Sift the spices with the flour. Add the citron. Beat the eggs, add the sugar and the remaining ingredients. Roll on board ¼ inch thick and cut into 2-by-3-inch squares. Lay on greased tins; let stand in cool place over night. Bake at 325 degrees F. for 25 minutes and frost with plain icing.

And here is a cheaper recipe, which we used during the war years:

Lebkuchen

4 whole eggs	1 tsp. cinnamon
1 lb. brown sugar	2 oz. citron, cut fine
2 cups flour	¼ lb. almonds or pecans

Beat eggs and sugar until fluffy. Mix flour and cinnamon with finely chopped nuts and citron; combine the two mixtures. Bake in two greased 10-by-15-inch pans in a moderate oven, 375 degrees F., for 25 minutes. Frost with plain icing.

Another typical cookie for the Christmas tree is called "Spanish Wind."

Spanish Wind

3 egg whites
¾ cup confectioners' sugar
1 tbsp. cornstarch

Beat whites until stiff. Add ¾ cup confectioners' sugar gradually; beat mixture until marshmallowy. Mix the cornstarch and remaining sugar and fold gently into the egg-white mixture. Put through pastry tube onto greased pan lined with waxed paper in the form of small wreaths. Bake in a slow oven, 275 degrees F., for 45 minutes.

Marzipan

1 lb. sweet almonds
¼ lb. bitter almonds
1¼ lbs. confectioners' sugar
2 egg whites, unbeaten

Blanch almonds, dry over night, grind very fine. Sift sugar over them, mix and knead to a stiff paste with the egg whites, or more egg, if needed. Roll with hands on board sprinkled with confectioners' sugar. Cut into pieces size of a walnut. Roll each piece ½ inch thick, form into rings, crescents, hearts, bow knots and pretzel shapes, and bake until slightly browned, in a moderately slow oven, 325 degrees F.

Most of these cookies are fastened with red string to the Christmas tree. In addition, there have to be trays and trays of small pastry ready to be eaten at random, like the following five recipes, each of which is a delicacy:

Rum Balls

½ lb. vanilla wafers	½ cup light corn syrup
2 tsp. cocoa	¼ cup rum or brandy
1 cup pecans, finely chopped	Confectioners' sugar

Grind wafers very fine. Add nuts, cocoa, syrup, and rum. Stir until well blended. Dust hands with confectioners' sugar and roll mixture into balls the size of a walnut. Let stand for about an hour to dry partially. Then roll in confectioners' sugar.

Nut Busserln

1 egg, beaten	1 cup chopped walnuts
1 cup sugar	5 tbsp. flour

Beat egg and sugar until very light; stir in chopped nuts, then add flour. Drop by teaspoonful on greased cookie sheet and bake in a moderate oven, 375 degrees F., about 10 minutes.

Cocoanut Busserln (Kisses)

2 egg whites
¼ lb. confectioners' sugar
¼ lb. shredded cocoanut

Beat the white of egg until stiff. Stir in the sugar well. Fold the shredded cocoanut in last. Drop mixture from tip of spoon ½ inch apart on greased cookie sheets. Bake in a slow oven, 250 degrees F., for 45 minutes. Remove from pan when slightly cool.

Rum Stangerln (Rum Slices)

4 egg whites	½ lb. walnuts, ground
1 lb. confectioners' sugar	1 tsp. vanilla
½ lb. pecans, ground	rum

Beat egg whites until stiff, add sugar and grated nuts. Flavor with vanilla or rum. Form into rolls ¾ inch in diameter. Chill for 45 minutes. Cut into ½ inch slices. Bake on greased tin in moderate oven, 350 degrees F., about 15 minutes. While still warm, ice with confectioners' sugar moistened with enough rum to spread.

Pfeffernuesse

2 cups corn syrup	1 tsp. soda
2 cups dark molasses	2 tsps. cinnamon
1 cup shortening	¼ lb. citron, cut fine
½ lb. brown sugar	¼ lb. almonds, chopped fine
10 cups flour	1 lemon, rind and juice

Warm syrup, add shortening and lemon juice and the remaining ingredients in order given, soda mixed with flour. Roll into little balls, brush with white of egg, place on greased pan far apart, and bake until brown, 350 degrees F. Roll in confectioners' sugar.

And then of course there must be quantities of just plain cookies. Here is our recipe:

Plain Cookies

½ cup shortening	¼ tsp. cream of tartar
1 egg	1½ cups flour
1 cup sugar	pinch of salt
½ tsp. baking powder	1 tsp. vanilla

Sift flour, baking powder, and cream of tartar. Cream shortening. Add sugar gradually, beating until fluffy. Add egg. Beat well. Then gradually add the flour mixture and flavoring. Roll into small balls. Set 1 inch apart on greased cookie sheet. Flatten. Sprinkle with sugar and cinnamon. Bake at 400 degrees F. about 10 to 12 minutes.

All through the 21st, 22nd, and 23rd, there is feverish activity in the kitchen. Tin after tin filled with cookies comes out of the oven, plates are piled high, *Kletzenbrot* and *Knörpeltorte* are finished, and kitchen and pantry look like a pastry shop. It is a sweet torture to smell these good aromatic perfumes and not to be allowed to taste even one, since in our house we abstain from cookies during Advent.

By midnight on the 23rd all must be finished. The dawn of the 24th finds a sober kitchen with all the goodies stored away and nothing left but the ingredients for a very frugal breakfast and lunch. Christmas Eve is one of the strictest fast days of the year. We have only a cup of coffee and a piece of dry bread for breakfast. For lunch, a bowl of fish salad stands on everyone's plate, and the only beverage is a glass of water. This is a special traditional fish salad, and here is the recipe:

Fish Salad

1½ cups cooked fish, flaked	2 hard-boiled egg yolks
1½ cups shrimp	½ cup whipped heavy cream
3 tsp. onion, grated	⅓ cup mayonnaise
1 cup thinly sliced celery	2 tsp. lemon juice

Combine fish, shrimp, onion and celery, season with salt and pepper. Sieve the egg yolks, mix with whipped cream, mayonnaise, and lemon juice. Combine the fish mixture with dressing. Serve in individual bowls lined with lettuce, garnish with a dash of paprika and a few capers. (This makes about eight servings.)

And with this lunch on Christmas Eve we have come to the end of the holy season of Advent. In the afternoon we begin the Vigil of Christmas.

Christmas

CHRISTMAS EVE

O N CHRISTMAS EVE in the morning the Church sang, "This day you shall know that the Lord is coming, and tomorrow you shall see His glory," and "Be ye lifted up, O eternal gates, and the King of glory shall enter in," and "The glory of the Lord shall be revealed, and all flesh together shall see, that the mouth of the Lord hath spoken."

These promises will be fulfilled during Midnight Mass.

It must be in order that the grown-ups may devote themselves with a quiet mind, unhindered by any commotion, to these great mysteries of the Holy Night, that in most Catholic countries the giving of gifts has been advanced to Christmas Eve. And so Christmas Eve is *the* day for our children. When the little ones get up in the morning, they find the door of the living room closed, and no one is allowed to go in, much less to peek through the keyhole; because the Christ Child will come and bring the Christmas tree and all the gifts. Only mother and father may assist Him.

Christmas Eve is Confession day. Once more we listen to the voice of St. John the Baptist, who admonishes us to prepare the way of the Lord and to do penance. When the Holy Child is entrusted into our hearts at midnight in our Christmas Communion, He shall find the place clean and swept and warm with love.

There is a certain hush all through the house. People are tip-toeing and whispering; at the same time there is an atmosphere of extreme activity. Mother and father spend the day behind the closed doors, "helping the Christ Child." In our house the large Christmas tree, twelve feet high, always a beautiful, thick balsam fir, requires a lot of time to be decorated "the old way." During the preceding nights, the older children have wrapped up candies in tinfoil or in tissue paper with fringed edges and have then tied red thread to candies as well as to hundreds of cookies. They are hung on the tree first. On the lower branches we hang also small apples and tangerines. Then come Christmas-tree decorations from our home studios—angels and stars worked in silver or brass, which will glitter later in the light of the candles. Yes, candles—because there will be six dozen small candleholders with real candles fastened to the branches. (On either side of the tree there will be a camouflaged bucket with water and a mop with a long handle "just in case." So far we have never needed it.) Next, dozens of packages of tinsel are emptied on twigs and branches; and the last touch is silver chains spinning in spider-web fashion, criss-crossed from branch to branch. The final effect is like a fairy tale.

Every so often the mother is interrupted by a discreet knock at the closed door and as she comes to open she can just hear steps running away. Everything and anything is a big secret today. As she opens the door just a little, she sees either a laundry basket or a cardboard box filled with many packages, each one with its name tag. So every one of the children comes with his gifts, for every one has prepared something for everybody else.

In a large household such as ours—when we are without guests we are eighteen—that means a great deal of arranging and rearranging until finally everything seems to be in its place. The last thing is to put the Christmas crib right next to the tree—the crib in the cold, dark cave where Mary and Joseph have arrived last night after evening prayers.

When, finally, everything in the "Christmas Room" (as the living room is called these days) is ready, the rest of the afternoon is devoted to tidying up the house. Not only the workshops and rooms, but also every drawer and closet is put in order. Then we all dress in

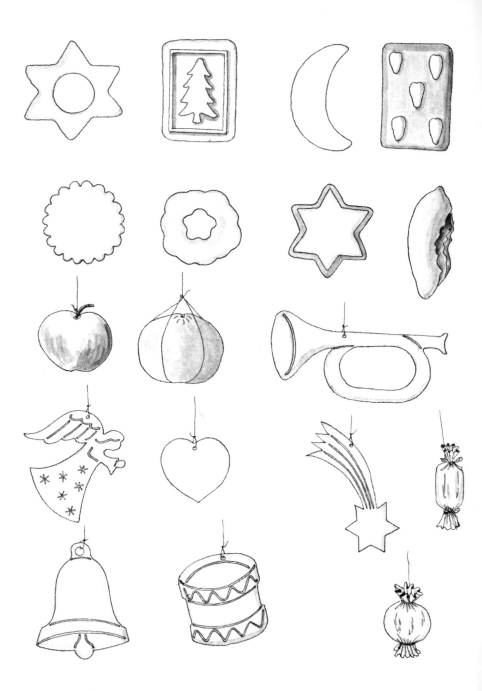

Decorations for Christmas Tree: Top two rows are various cookie samples for the tree; third row, apple and tangerine; next six items can be cut from heavy tin foil or aluminum foil, which is available in various colors. Use knitting needle to scratch details into figures. Bottom right: samples of candy wrappings. Use colored tissue paper, tie with colored string.

our feast-day best. When it gets dusky outside, we meet in the chapel. (Before we had our chapel, we used to meet in a big bedroom upstairs.) Besides the vigil light, there is only the little flame of the Advent candle burning. We say the rosary, and afterwards we sing every one of our Advent hymns and at the end a song to the Blessed Mother. When we are in the middle of it, one can hear clearly the ringing of a little silver bell. A suppressed sigh can be heard coming from the little ones. This is their hour, because the bell announces that the Christ Child has come. Now we all go downstairs, and the double doors of the living room are wide open. A big Christmas tree stands there all ablaze in the light of many candles. Tables covered with white cloths are heaped with beautifully wrapped packages—gifts put there by love. First the youngest in the family steps forward and recites the Nativity story according to St. Luke. Then we sing for the first time "Silent Night"—three verses in German and in English. (For the first time at home, that is. We have sung it many times in our Christmas programs during the last weeks, always anticipating this moment when it would be sung at home.) And then everyone wishes everyone else, not a "Merry," but a "Blessed Christmas": "*Gesegnete Weihnachten.*" After this the mother leads everybody to his or her place and, for the next hour, the room is filled with happy exclamations.

Then the bell rings for an early supper. This, again, is traditional: carp with potato salad and, as dessert, *Knörpeltorte.*

Afterwards, there is still a little lingering in the Christmas room and then—also according to tradition—everybody lies down to catch a little sleep before Midnight Mass. Around eight o'clock the house is dark and silent.

The first one who gets up is the father. When he is fully dressed in his heavy winter coat, he takes a lantern containing a burning candle and stands all by himself in the hall and starts singing an old Christmas carol that is only sung once a year. We never sing it earlier, and we never repeat it afterwards.

SHEPHERDS, UP!

Austrian Carol, traditional.

Shep - herds, up, your watch to take! Your time of
sleep is end - ing, for the Good Shep - herd
is a - wake, His earth-ly flock at - tend - ing.
Haste to the man-ger, to Ma - ry, so mild,
Come and a - dore Him, the heav-en-ly Child!

As all through the house the bedroom doors are opening, the family one by one come down and join the father in the song. Everyone comes ready to go and everyone carries his lantern. There we stand now and sing verse after verse—each verse a tone higher—until all of us have gathered. And then we go out into ice and snow—be-

cause in Austria as well as in Vermont, there is always a white
Christmas (or almost always)—to the little village church for Midnight Mass.

Stowe in Vermont being every bit as cold as Austria (and sometimes much colder), this trip always reminds us very much of Christmas in the old home. There it was about a ten-minute walk to the
little church of Aigen bei Salzburg, a village surrounded by mountains. We always used to linger a little bit in front of the church,
listening to the strains of "Silent Night" and "Oh, du Fröhliche,"
played on horns from the church steeple, and watching the many
little sparks coming down the mountains—the people carrying
torches and lanterns. It looked as if stars were walking down the
mountainside—a lovely picture.

Now in our new home, "Cor Unum," in Stowe, Vermont, we do it
this way: As the church is three miles away, we do not walk there;
but once in a while it happens that the road leading up our hill is
coated with ice. Then, on the way home from Midnight Mass we
leave the cars at the foot of the hill and walk up. This is a real treat.
Parts of the road go through the woods, and as we climb up the hill,
the snow squeaking at every step, the stars seem to glitter much
brighter than on any other night, and the cold, crisp winter air seems
to be saturated with that peace which has been particular to the
Christmas season ever since the first Christmas when the angel an-
nounced it: ". . . and peace on earth to men of good will."

At home there awaits us another treat. Supper has been early, and
everyone is hungry by now, so first there are hot boiled frankfurters
with dark rye bread, and then the famous Christmas punch, served
with Christmas *Stollen.* This is the way we make the punch:

Christmas Punch

1 sliced pineapple	1 lb. sugar
1 bottle claret	grated rind of 1 lemon
1 bottle red wine	grated rind of 1 orange
½ bottle rum	4 whole oranges cut in pieces
juice of 4 lemons	1 stick cinnamon, broken up
juice of 4 oranges	1 vanilla bean
1 pint water	½ cup maraschino cherries

Boil spices thoroughly with the water. Remove them and pour the water into large earthenware pot. Add lemon and orange and rind, as well as pineapple and sugar (fruit and sugar prepared in a separate dish). Then add wine and rum, cover and heat. Add champagne before serving.

This is strictly for the grownups. The children in the family get another punch:

Christmas Punch for Children

1 qt. grape juice	1 stick cinnamon
2 qts. water	juice of 2 lemons
2 cups sugar	juice of 2 oranges
½ tsp. whole cloves	rind of above lemons and oranges

Boil sugar, water, lemon rind, and spices until flavored. Mix with the rest of the ingredients, boil five minutes, and serve hot in punch glasses.

And here is the recipe for the Christmas *Stollen:*

Stollen

4 cups flour	½ tsp. nutmeg
2 cups lukewarm milk	1 lb. butter, softened
1 tsp. salt	¾ lb. raisins
2 cakes compressed yeast or 2 packages dry granular yeast	¼ cup rum
	½ lb. chopped almonds
	grated rind of 1 lemon
1 cup sugar	½ cup each orange peel and citron, cut fine
4 whole eggs	

Mix the yeast and milk, and stir in 1 cup flour. Let rise. Cream butter with sugar, add eggs, one at a time, and beat well. Add lemon rind and salt; combine the two mixtures, add flour, nutmeg, and knead until smooth and elastic. Sprinkle flour over the dried fruits. Mix and add to the dough with nuts and rum. Let rise until double its bulk. Toss on floured board. Divide into three or more loaves. Roll out slightly, spread top with melted butter, press down the center, and fold over double. Brush melted butter over top, let rise until doubled, and bake in a moderate oven, 350 degrees F., about 45 minutes. When slightly cool, cover with plain icing.

This get-together after Midnight Mass in the Christmas Room, which is filled with that indescribable "Christmas smell"—compounded of wax candles, *Lebkuchen*, and balsam fir—has such a very special quality that even the word *gemütlich* becomes inadequate. It is hard to tear oneself away from the Christmas tree and the presents. The children, big and small alike, take the favorite present along to bed.

FROM HEAVEN HIGH, O ANGELS, COME

Text and melody, 17th century. The two parts written on the second stave may be sung (soprano and alto, or alto and tenor) or played on any instruments.

pipe and drum, Al - le - lu - ia, al - le - lu -

ia. Of Je- sus sing and Ma - ri - a.

2. Let every instrument join in,
   Eya, eya, susani, susani, susani.
   Bring lute and harp and violin,
   Alleluia, alleluia. Of Jesus sing and Maria.

3. Send forth your voices louder yet,
   Eya, eya, susani, susani, susani.
   With organ and with flageolet,
   Alleluia, alleluia. Of Jesus sing and Maria.

4. How heavenly must the music be,
   Eya, eya, susani, susani, susani.
   Because a heavenly Child is He,
   Alleluia, alleluia. Of Jesus sing and Maria.

5. To men on earth all peace may be,
   Eya, eya, susani, susani, susani.
   And praise to God eternally,
   Alleluia, alleluia. Of Jesus sing and Maria.

O INFANT, GOD'S ETERNAL SON
Well known since 1623.

O In - fant, God's e - ter - nal Son, O

man - ger, tru - ly So - lo - mon's throne. O

sta - ble, beau - teous pa - ra - dise,

straw like ro - ses with - out price. Child in

ox - en - stall, Make us ho - ly all.

In - fant in the hay, Make us gay!

2. O Child, Thou art beyond compare,
Thy Face as bright as roses fair,
Thou art all fair from head to feet,
And more than rarest honey sweet.
Child in oxen stall,
Make us holy all.
Infant in the hay,
Make us gay.

3. *Thy tiny form is ivory white,*
   With glowing sapphire all alight,
   The sapphire Thy divinity,
   The ivory, sweet humanity.—Refrain

4. *Within Thy breast a light divine*
   With love toward every heart doth shine,
   No joy of heaven can e'er replace
   The joy of those who see Thy Face.—Refrain

CHRISTMAS DAY

It is not a very long night, however. The morning finds us in chapel again. After the "Angel Mass" at midnight, we return to the manger, together with the simple guardians of the sheep, to the "Shepherds' Mass," which should be said at dawn, to be followed at broad daylight by a Solemn High Mass. It is as if the great mystery of the Incarnation could not be contemplated enough in just one Holy Mass. The threefold coming of Christ, for which we have been praying and waiting for weeks, we like to celebrate in a threefold way. Already the little children get a sense of the immense importance and mystery of the day when they are summoned to church three times instead of once.

Afterwards, one is "holily tired," as one of our little girls once said, and ready for Christmas dinner, which brings the traditional goose done "just so."

Dessert for Christmas dinner is the plum pudding, carried in ablaze with the lights turned out.

In the evening of Christmas Day we gather in the Christmas Room, light the tree again, and sing Christmas carols to our hearts' delight.

FROM CHRISTMAS TO NEW YEAR

When we lived in Austria, the three greatest feasts of the year were distinguished by two church holidays each: Easter Sunday and Easter Monday, Pentecost Sunday and Pentecost Monday, and St. Stephen's Day after Christmas Day. We know that the war did away with these second Church holidays, but they still exist in our memory and we always keep them in our house. In Austria the peasants used to celebrate St. Stephen's Day in a special way, because St. Stephen is the patron saint for horses, watching over their health. After the Solemn High Mass the pastor would come in surplice and stole and wait in front of the church door with holy water and sprinkler. The horses of the village, beautifully decorated with ribbons in their manes and tails, would now parade before him in solemn procession and he would bless every single one of them. He would also bless oats and hay, which each farmer had brought along for that purpose; the horses would be fed with the blessed feed, to protect them against sickness and accidents.

According to tradition, St. John the Apostle was once presented by his enemies with a cup of poisoned wine intended to kill him. When the Apostle made the sign of the cross over the wine, however, the cup split in half and the poisoned wine was spilled. In memory of this, the Church has a special blessing, the "Benedictio Sancti Johannes." On the 27th, the feast of St. John, the people bring wine along to church and before Holy Mass the priest blesses it. At the main meal at home the wine is poured into as many glasses as there are people. Just before the meal begins, everybody stands up, holding his glass, while the father and mother begin the St. John's Day ceremony: The father touches the mother's glass with his glass, looks her in the eyes and says, "I drink to you the love of St. John." The mother answers, "I thank you for the love of St. John," and they both take a sip. Then the mother turns to the oldest child and repeats, "I drink to you the love of St. John," and the child answers, "I thank you for the love of St. John." Again they take a sip and the child turns to the next oldest, and so it goes around the table until the last one turns to the father and the family circle is closed. Some of the blessed wine is kept for days of sickness or of great celebration. If someone in the family is about to take a journey, a few drops of the blessed wine are added to each wine glass and the whole family again drinks "the love of St. John." Immediately after the wedding ceremony, the newly-wed couple also drink to each other "the love of St. John."

The day following St. John's Day is a great day for the children. This goes back to a medieval custom in monastery schools: On December 28th, the day dedicated to the Holy Innocents, the boys used to elect one from their midst as bishop—"the Episcopus Puerorum." This boy-bishop would take over the direction of the abbey for this one day. Dressed in pontifical vestments, surrounded by his schoolmates, he would sit in the place of the abbot and the others in the choir stalls of the monks, whereas abbot and monks moved over to the places of the pupils. This custom is still alive in many convents and monasteries, where the young ones in the novitiate have the ruling of the house for this particular day. It also is preserved in many families, where the little ones take the seats of the father and mother and try to play a few little tricks on the grownups as long as they are in authority.

December 31st, the last day of the old year, or New Year's Eve, finds the whole family in the Christmas Room again. In the morning there was a Thanksgiving Mass, solemnly starting the day. Looking back over the past three hundred and sixty-five days with their bright and their dark hours, we gave thanks for both the bright and the dark to Him Who knows what is best for us. In some parts of the old country the people observe a strict fast and abstinence during this day (which in earlier times was observed solemnly throughout Christendom) as a token of its serious, thought-provoking character.

NEW YEAR'S EVE

In our day, however, New Year's Eve is dedicated to fun and merry-making. Part of the fun consists in getting a glimpse of what the new year is going to bring. All kinds of old superstitions are still alive, and although no one believes in them, everyone joins in the fun. One sure way of finding out what you are going to do in the new year is by "lead-pouring." The party gathers around the fireplace, where, in an iron ladle, pieces of old lead pipe are molten. (Any notion-counter carries lead buttons, if pipes are unavailable!) You hold the ladle over the open fire and, when the lead is liquid, you pour it into a bucket filled with cold water. The lead will stiffen in all kinds of strange shapes. There are several soothsayers in the family who have acquired a knack for deciphering the lead language. With incredible skill they will inform you that your piece of lead really has the shape of a sailing boat (or locomotive, or the side view of a car), which indicates that you are going to make a journey soon. (How astonishing—with a concert tour always just around the corner!) Then there are distinct signs of a letter which is already in the mail, full of surprises (how very likely—if your daily mail brings thirty to forty letters). Then, and now you are really warming up to it, there's money coming! Then you are warned: There is somebody who doesn't like you (not really—how is that possible?); on the other hand, you are lucky because somebody loves you very much, although he keeps it hidden. Finally the young soothsayer concludes his analysis of your New Year with these consoling words: You can be satisfied, as there is much to look forward to!

When all the lead is poured and everyone has a good inkling of what to expect in the coming year, we play games.

"Let's play the handkerchief game!" someone will suggest.

There we all sit in a large circle on the floor. A clean handkerchief is tied up in knots so that it takes the shape of a ball and can be thrown easily through the air. Hedwig volunteers to go out. Now we start throwing the handkerchief across the circle. We have to keep it going until Hedwig comes in. At the moment of her entrance, the one who has just caught it will have to hide it, and Hedwig will have to guess where the handkerchief is. She gives three warning knocks at the door, but as we know that immediately after the third she will burst through the door, we are getting increasingly nervous between the second and third warnings. Sometimes it leads to hilarious situations. The moment Hedwig steps into the room, everyone's features relax into complete, harmless innocence. Everyone's face spells: "Handkerchief? I don't know what you are talking about, Hedwig!" Hedwig has three guesses. If she hasn't found out after the third one, she has to go out again. But this rarely happens. Some people blush helpfully, others look like bad conscience personified, wiggling nervously on the handkerchief they are trying to hide by sitting on it. Everyone—guests, grownups, and children—has to be in on the game. And of course, the one who has been discovered hiding the handkerchief has to go out next.

From long years of experience I know that one should stop every game when it is at its height. Never let it wear thin. So I suggest "Jump at Quotations" and I'm always met with eager consent. Last New Year's Eve the children took three quotations from my little speeches on the stage: "Are you a tenor or a bass?" "And I am the mother!" "The family who plays together and prays together usually stays together."

The teams are placed at opposite sides of the room. Each team gets the same quotation. One word of the quotation gets pinned to the back of each player. At "Go" one may read the word on the back of every other member of one's team, but not that on one's own back. Rule: No oral communication! The winning team is the one that first gets itself lined up in correct order. (Have the words in large-size printing so the "audience" can enjoy the fun too!)

And then there is the treasure hunt. Everyone gets a list of objects that have been placed in plain sight in the Christmas Room. After it has been explained to the guests that the object of the game is to locate all of the "treasures" as quickly as possible and note them down on one's own list, and after the rule has been stressed that nothing can be touched, the signal to "Go" is given. This was last year's list, which by chance I kept:

a cherry (on top of lampshade)
an olive (on a branch of the Christmas tree)
dry noodles (woven into wicker chair)
soap (on piano key)
an egg (in a light socket, instead of a bulb)
lump of sugar (on ceiling light)
toothbrush (over picture frame)
clothes pin (on lampshade)
picture of "Mother Trapp" (pasted on book jacket)
2-cent stamp (on pink book jacket, in bookshelf)
onion (on window sill)
"Cheerios" (in carving of chest)

In the margin of my list I had scribbled, "Funny, how blind people are!"

The time given to find the treasures was twenty minutes. And out of fifty-four participants, only three found every item!

The next game has to be tried in order to be appreciated. It is called a "Smiling Contest." There are two teams, two judges, two tape measures. Each judge has a tape measure, pencil, and paper. One person from each team comes forward. A judge then measures the width of his smile and records it (one judge per team). The next pair come forward and are measured in turn, until every smile has been measured. The judges then add up the total yards of smiles for each team. The higher total wins, and it is interesting to see who has the biggest smile, too. The funny effect is in the two simultaneous smiles, each trying to outdo the other!

Then voices are heard: "Let's sing some more carols!" Invariably Father Wasner's voice will interrupt right here: "First we are going to sing the New Year's song!" And there we go: "From heaven through the clouds on high."

The very character of the evening lends itself to gay Christmas songs. There are many in Austrian dialect dealing with the astonished shepherds who cannot believe their eyes during Holy Night.

As eleven o'clock nears, someone will suggest, "Let's sing a few lullabies." They always seem to be the very heart of our carol-singing. Several are in Tyrolean dialect. Here we give some of our favorites.

Close to eleven o'clock, Agathe and Maria will disappear into the kitchen, soon to return with trays of "Sylvester Punch." (In Austria the last day of the year is dedicated to the Holy Pope, St. Sylvester, who baptized Constantine the Great, thereby bringing about the dawning not only of the New Year but of a new era; for this reason, the night before the New Year is called *Sylvesterabend* (Eve of St. Sylvester).

Sylvester Punch

> Red burgundy (count one bottle for six people)
> Equal amount of hot tea
> 12 cloves
> rind of 1 lemon
> 2 tbsp. sugar to each bottle of wine
> 2 cinnamon sticks to each bottle of wine

Pour the liquid into an enamel pot, add the cloves, the thinly pared rind of 1 lemon, the sugar, and the cinnamon. Heat over a low flame but do not allow to boil. At the last moment add the tea. Serve hot.

If there are many children and very young people, it is good to know different fruit punch combinations. Here is a basic recipe, with variations:

> ½ cup lemon juice   grated rind of 1 lemon
> 1 cup orange juice   1 qt. water
> grated rind of ½ orange   1 cup sugar

Cook sugar and water for five minutes. Cool. Add juices and the grated rind and any of the following combinations:

(1) 1 cup grated pineapple, 1 qt. ginger ale.
(2) 1 qt. strained, sweetened strawberry juice, 1 qt. raspberry juice, 2 qts. ginger ale.
(3) 1 glass currant jelly dissolved in 1 cup hot water. Cook, chill, and add ¼ cup mint, finely minced.
(4) 1 qt. cider, 1 qt. grape juice, 1 qt. soda water.

It is great fun to try out new variations every year. One starts with lemonade or orangeade and soon the children will go on to pineapple-ade, raspberry-ade. . . . In our family we have something called "Hedwig-ade" because it is Hedwig's own secret.

SONG FOR THE NEW YEAR

Leonhard Lechner, 1553-1606. Translation by Hester Root.
The original composition is for five parts. They are here reduced
to two parts.

ne — ver cease!

ne — ver cease!

CHILD JESUS SO DEAR

Text of first verse, Hymn Book, Cologne, 1623; of second and
third verse, Hymn Book, Strassburg, 1697. Melody more recent.

Child Je - sus so dear, Thy man-ger is bare, O

Je - sus so dear, so hard and so bare. Ah, take Thy

ease and Thy cry - ing now cease, Sleep and

grant us e - ter - nal peace, e - ter - nal peace!

2. *Winds, silence now keep and let the Child sleep!*
   All breezes away, that slumber he may.—Refrain
3. *No movement is heard, no creature has stirred,*
   His eyelids now close in tender repose.—Refrain

THE VIRGIN'S LULLABYE

Tyrolean. The text should be sung by an alto voice, the soprano hums the obbligato, which can also be played by a
violin, flute, or recorder.

VERY SLOW AND MEDITATIVELY

Thy dear cheeks, my Child, are ro-sy red, My love for

Thee is strong as death. And in Thy cheeks a-glow are

dim-ples fine, Thou art and shalt be ev-er mine. Brightly

shine Thine eyes and they are heav'nly blue, There's none more

sweet   the whole world through.   Thy dear cheeks, my Child,   are

ros - y   red,   My love for   Thee   is strong as   death.

2. Thy dear lips, my Child, are honey sweet,
   When Thee I kiss, when Thee I greet.
   And Thy darling hands are snowy white,
   They are my joy, my heart's delight.
   Thy two feet are tiny, they are soft,
   They shall me guide to heaven aloft.
   Guardian angels round Thy bed so bright,
   I sing to Thee a sweet "Good Night."

After the punch is brought in, we form a circle and everybody raises his glass. Then we say, in a chorus, "Happy New Year." From there we go up to the chapel, because for the last half hour of the old year and the first of the new year everyone wants to stand alone with his God. There is much to think back on, much to be sorry for, and how we wish we could relive parts of the old year, because we would do it differently now. . . . But this has to be commended to the mercy of God with a heartfelt act of contrition. On the other hand, there is so much to be grateful for in the spiritual and the physical order of our life. This Holy Hour around midnight, starting at half past eleven and lasting to twelve-thirty, is so timed that Father Wasner lifts the monstrance in Benediction at the moment the clock strikes twelve.

Before we had a chapel, we held the same Holy Hour right there at the Christmas crib, and when the clock struck twelve we got up from our knees and sang "Holy God We Praise Thy Name," remaining a little while afterwards, each one according to his need. The last moments of the old year and the first moments of the new year are sanctified by Our Lord's blessing.

From this Holy Hour everyone goes quietly to bed.

NEW YEAR'S DAY

Although the night was rather short, nobody wants to stay in bed long on New Year's Day because there is an old belief that everything you do on the first of January is an indication of how you will behave throughout the next year. If you are late on New Year's morning, that's bad. You will be late most of the days to come. So every child tries to be his most charming best. . . .

In the liturgy the beginning of the new year is not commemorated. The Mass texts of New Year's Day are a combination of three different thoughts: the Circumcision of the Infant Jesus, the octave of Christmas, and some texts taken from the Votive Mass of the Blessed Virgin Mary. Thus there is a great likelihood that the priest once said three Masses on this day.

New Year's dinner is a big occasion. This is the day of the suckling pig, the little pig being one of the good luck symbols. The family table is decorated with little pigs made of marzipan, chocolate, maple sugar, fudge, or cookie dough. Besides the pig, there is also the four-leaf clover, and, in Austria, the chimney sweep. As the recipe for the roast suckling pig might not be generally known, here it is:

Roast Suckling Pig

Clean the pig carefully. Insert a piece of wood into its mouth to keep it open while roasting.

You may use sage and onion dressing, which would taste more American, but we always use the old Austrian apple stuffing. (We have heard of people there who used to stuff their pigs with sausages, but that is awfully rich.)

Now stuff the pig, truss and skewer it. Make four parallel incisions about four inches long on each side of the backbone. Place it on a rack, sprinkle it with salt and some pepper, brush thoroughly with melted butter, and dust with flour.

Roast for 15 minutes at 480 degrees. Then reduce to 350. Continue roasting, allowing 30 minutes to the pound. If you wish to have the skin soft, baste every 15 minutes with hot stock. If you want it crisp (we think it is much better that way), baste with melted butter. When the roast is ready, remove to a hot serving platter. Now remove the piece of wood from the mouth, replace with a bright red apple, and insert cranberries for eyes. Finally crown with a wreath of bay leaves. Be careful to wrap the ears and the tail during the roasting in buttered paper, which you remove only the last half hour. Otherwise they easily burn.

The dessert, after the roast pig, is green peppermint ice cream in the shape of a four-leaf clover.

THE FEAST OF THE HOLY NAME OF JESUS

On the Sunday after New Year's Day the Church celebrates the feast of the Holy Name of Jesus.

"But, Mother, this is Our Lord's feast day!" And Lorli, aged five, looked as if she had made a big discovery.

"We have to celebrate it—but how? Do you think Our Lord would like His monogram used as a table decoration?" asked Martina, who had just in that year copied beautifully the "I.H.S." in genuine gold-leaf on a deep cornflower-blue background.

And so it was done. The monogram of the name of Jesus was put as centerpiece on the table, surrounded by flowers. We happened to have company on that day and somebody asked, pointing to the golden letters, "What is that?" And so we told the story:

Around 1400 there lived in Italy a holy Franciscan monk by the name of Bernardin. From the name of his home town, he became famous as Bernardin of Siena, and famous he became for his great eloquence. He was the most renowned preacher of his days and he always had a great love and admiration for the Holy Name of Jesus. Soon his fame had spread all over Italy, and people came from far distances to hear Bernardin preach. All the churches were too small to accommodate the crowds. In Siena he had to use the big piazza. There was one great vice prevalent in his town at that time: card-playing. Every night the men spent all their time and money gambling, and the women did not know how to keep the fathers of the family at home and how to prevent the household money from being gambled away; so they went to St. Bernardin and asked him to do something about it.

On the next Sunday, when the piazza was jammed with people as usual, Bernardin got up in his improvised pulpit and preached with so much fervor against card-playing that the people were deeply affected. At the end of his sermon he asked them to bring their packs of playing cards and put them on a pile in the middle of the piazza, and they really did so, until there was a large pyramid of playing cards. The Saint lit a candle from the vigil light of the altar and set fire to the pile. As he turned around, a man approached him, tears streaming down his cheeks. "Padre," he wailed, "and what is to become of me?" And he informed the

Saint that he was the man who had manufactured the cards. "How shall I earn a living now? I'm facing starvation if no one buys my cards any more." The Saint looked startled for a moment. This had never occurred to him. He closed his eyes and sent a silent, fervent prayer to Our Lord asking for enlightenment. When he opened his eyes again, he smiled at the man and said, "Give me a board and a piece of chalk." When the man had produced both, St. Bernardin drew, in the lettering of his time, the letters "I.H.S." (from the Latin *"Jesus Hominum Salvator"* meaning "Jesus, Saviour of men"). "Print this instead," said the Saint, handing the board to the man. "Golden letters on a blue background, and have them ready next week."

And on the next Sunday, when all the people had returned bringing friends along until there was not a square foot left on the huge piazza, the Saint gave his famous sermon on the efficacy of the Name of Jesus and how we should carry it with us, how we should place it in our rooms over our bed, in our prayer books, over the house doors, how we should carry it in the form of a medal around the neck because it is the monogram of the Name of Him Whom we should love more than anybody or anything else. The people took this advice, and the little man who had formerly sold playing cards sold from now on the famous monogram, which soon appeared cut in stone, carved in wood, modelled in clay, printed on paper, used in illuminations, and which is decorating our table today because of the feast of the Holy Name which it represents.

EPIPHANY

In earlier times there were twelve holy nights between Christmas and Epiphany—called "Smoke Nights," because the people went through their houses and barns burning incense, blessing their homestead. Only one such night is left, but this is celebrated with great solemnity: the Vigil of Epiphany, January 5th. After the supper dishes are done, the whole family, dressed in Sunday clothes, follow the father, who goes ahead with a shovel of charcoal on which he burns incense, while the oldest son has a bowl with holy water—Epiphany water, blessed with a much longer formula than the ordinary holy water, a formula that contains a prolonged exorcism, which makes it efficacious against all demoniacal influence—which he sprinkles freely all over house and grounds and barns, while the rest of the family follow behind, saying the rosary and singing hymns. While the father and the oldest son are incensing and blessing the house, the youngest child carries on a plate a piece of chalk. This has been blessed with a special blessing from the Rituale after the morning Mass. In the old country every household would be most careful to send somebody into church for the blessing of the chalk. At the very end, when the whole homestead had been blessed, room by room, the father took the blessed chalk and wrote over every room that led from the house into the open:

AD 19 C M B 55

which stands for "Anno Domini 1955—Caspar, Melchior, Balthasar" and means that the three Holy Kings, Caspar, Melchior, and Balthasar, in this year of Our Lord, 1955 (or whatever the year may be), are protecting this house against all evil spirits.

Epiphany is also known as "Little Christmas." As a feast it is even much older than our Christmas. On the Vigil, the eve before the feast, there comes to the table a special Epiphany cake, in which three beans are hidden—two white ones, one black one. Whoever gets a bean in his piece has to dress up next day as a Holy King. The one who got the dark bean will be the black King. (Soot from the fireplace or black shoe polish are recommended.) On Epiphany Day the three Holy Kings, with golden crowns and richly dressed in oriental splendor, are the guests of honor at the table. Afterwards the whole family tries to entertain them and they have the say of the evening. This is always an evening much looked forward to by the whole house. We have had the most fantastic-looking magi at our table. Before the three majesties leave the house again, they hand over their gifts—equivalents for gold, incense, and myrrh.

CANDLEMAS

All through the month of January the crèche is standing in the living room, even if the Christmas tree has been removed, and every night the family prayers will be said beside the crib, followed by at least one Christmas song.

When Holy Mother Church came to Rome, in the time of the Apostles, she found that the Roman women went around town with torches and other lights on February 1st in honor of the goddess Ceres. The Church continued the same custom but "baptized" it: Forty days after the birth of a child the Jewish mother had to be purified in the temple, and so we celebrate on February 2nd the Purification of Mary and the Presentation of her little Son in the Temple; this should be celebrated in the light of many candles, in honor of Him of Whom the old Simeon said on that day, "He shall illumine the Gentiles with His light and shall be the glory of the people of Israel." There was a special blessing for the water on Epiphany Day, and there is a special solemn blessing for the candles

ANTIPHON FOR CANDLEMAS DAY

Recite the Canticle of Simeon (Luke 2, 29-32) and repeat the Antiphon after each verse.

A Light to the re - ve - la - tion of the Gen - tiles: and the glo - ry of Thy peo - ple Is - ra - el.

on this Candlemas Day. Besides having beautiful prayers, the Church helps us to understand the symbolism of the light blessed on this day, so that we may make the right use of it by the bed of the dying, during storms, and in all perils to which may be exposed "our bodies and souls on land and on the waters." The five special prayers of Candlemas Day are so beautiful and so full of meaning that they should be read aloud as evening prayer the night before and explained by parents to their children.

On Candlemas Day every family should carry home a blessed candle, which will have a special place on the home altar and will be lit in all moments of danger, during thunderstorms, during sickness, in time of tribulation.

Candlemas Day is a bitter-sweet feast. While in the morning the church is bathed in the light of hundreds of candles in the hands of the faithful, afterwards the crèche is stored again. It marks the end of the Christmas season; and the sheep and shepherds, the Gloria angel, the ox and the ass, Mary and Joseph with the Infant, and the whole little town of Bethlehem are hidden away for another year. There is always a tinge of sadness in the air, because, during these long nine weeks, the Holy Family has become so much a part of our household that it is hard to see them go.

HAIL MARY, QUEEN IN HEAV'N ENTHRONED

From the evening of Candlemas to Easter this Antiphon is
sung instead of "Blessed Mother of the Saviour."

Hail Ma - ry, Queen in Heav'n en - throned Hail Thou,
Mis - tress by all an - gels owned! Root of Jes - se, Hail, Gate
of Morn, the world's true light from Thee was born.
Vir - gin glo - rious, ev - er fair - est, of all
crea - tures to Him near - est. Hail to Thee, hal - lowed in
Heav - en! May Thy child - ren's guilt be for - giv - en.

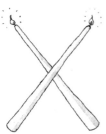

Carnival

SAINT CATHERINE closes the door of the dance hall until the three Holy Kings throw it wide open again," is a saying in the Catholic countries. This means that with the feast of St. Catherine (November 25th), the Church enters the "closed time." In these weeks good Christians are not allowed to attend public dances and are not supposed to have a big festive wedding celebration.

There are two such closed times—between November 25th and Christmas, and again between Ash Wednesday and Easter Sunday. In former times the weeks of Advent were called "the little Lent," and the people fasted almost as carefully as they would in the "big Lent." ("Big" only because it lasted longer.)

Fasting during the "little Lent" is all but forgotten now, but the character of this closed time is still very much respected in Catholic countries.

In order to make up for these two periods of abstinence from dancing and merry-making, there is sandwiched in between a time that is, on the contrary, even dedicated to dancing and feasting of any kind. In Austria these weeks are called *Fasching*. In Latin countries they are known by the name of *Carnevale*. The Latin name is usually translated as "Meat—farewell!" ("*Carne—Vale!*"). As we know, one main feature of fasting is usually abstinence from meat.

84

Here in the United States we have come across the word "Carnival" almost exclusively in connection with the Mardi Gras celebration in New Orleans, so that people have the idea that Carnival is celebrated only on the day before Ash Wednesday ("Mardi Gras," or "Fat Tuesday"). This, however, is not so. Carnival is a season extending over several weeks. It is not equally long each year, depending on whether Easter falls earlier or later; but it always begins January 6th and ends at midnight before Ash Wednesday.

Nobody could stand a Thanksgiving Day dinner every day of the year. There can only be mountains if there are also valleys. It is a pity that the Reformation did away not only with most of the sacraments and all of the sacramentals, but also, unfortunately, with the very breath of the Mystical Body—that wonderful, eternal rhythm of high and low tide that makes up the year of the Church: times of waiting alternate with times of fulfillment, the lean weeks of Lent with the feasts of Easter and Pentecost, times of mourning with seasons of rejoicing. Modern man lost track of this. Deep down in the human heart, however, is imbedded the craving to celebrate, and, in a dumb way, the other craving to abstain, perhaps to atone. In general, these cravings are no longer directed in seasonal channels, as they are for the Catholic, or even for the aborigine who participates in some tribal religious belief. So modern man one day—any day—gets up and says, "Let's celebrate!" And without any warrant, he decrees that his town from now on will have a festival on, let's say, August 18th; and as he can dance and eat and drink on any day between January 1st and December 31st, the most he will experience is "a good time." But he will never be able to "celebrate a feast."

It should be our noble right and duty to bring up our children in such a way that they become conscious of high tide and low tide, that they learn that there is "a time to weep, and a time to laugh, a time to mourn, and a time to dance." The rhythm of nature as it manifests itself in the four seasons, in day and night, in the individual's heartbeat and breathing—this rhythm we should learn to recognize, and to treat with more reverence. Modern man has become used to turning day into night and night into day according to his whim or pleasure. He has managed to lose contact completely with himself. He has lost the instinct for the right food and drink, stuffing himself with huge quantities of the wrong things and feeding himself sick. But worst of all, and this sounds almost ridiculous, in the process of growing up he forgot the right kind of breathing. Only babies nowadays know how to breathe. Every voice teacher can prove this sad truth.

Again, it is our faithful friend, Holy Mother Church, who leads her children first back to nature in order to make them ready to receive supernatural grace. *"Gratia supponit naturam."*

Looked upon in this light, the weeks of Carnival are a most necessary time for the individual as well as for families and communities. This period is set aside for us to "let off steam," "to have a good time." And for this we need company. Therefore, Carnival is most obviously the season for parties and family get-togethers, to which the married children come home as they do for Thanksgiving Day dinner —with the avowed intention of having that good time *together.* (Children who grew up this way and for whom Carnival has become a cherished tradition will always gladly return once a year for this happy purpose.) Carnival is the time to be social, to give and to receive invitations for special parties. It is the time to celebrate as a parish group, perhaps once every week, maybe on Sunday afternoon. Again, from long experience, I must say: All these parties must have someone who plans and shapes them and—very important —terminates them. It is a requirement for a successful party to know when to stop. "Whoever feasts too long gets disillusioned," said an old proverb, and "A little less would have been more" is the verdict on many an unsuccessful social event. Therefore, one person, or a small committee (*small,* mind you!), should make the plans: where to meet and when, for how long, what to eat and drink, and what the topic of the evening will be.

There seems to be something in human nature that makes us want to dress up once in a great while, to pretend to be somebody else (and this is true not only of children). As our family is so large, we were always self-sustaining when it came to celebrating feasts. The most hilarious evenings were those when we all came in fancy dress.

It helps greatly if there is a theme to the evening, such as "Whom I Would Like to Be" or "International Evening" (many nationalities and people are chosen by lot and have to be represented; and for the first half hour sign language is obligatory). Or "A Get-Together of Our Great-Grandchildren in the year 2,000" or "Circus" (everyone comes as an active member, human or animal, of a travelling circus), or . . . or. . . . There is no end to good ideas. The main thing is that everyone should take over a rôle and play it the whole evening, within the general frame of the theme. And there is a deeper meaning in all this, too—because everyone would like to be somebody else once in a while.

It would not be Carnival without dancing. Mankind has danced since before the time of King David, and always will; for it seems to be an irreplaceable means of expression—the one way in which the whole person, body and soul, can enjoy the beauty of rhythm. And now we should ask ourselves this question, especially if we are young people: What do we know about the dance and its function in the history of mankind? Have we ever been privileged to witness a dance festival among the Pueblo Indians? And I do not mean one arranged for the tourists—I mean one of their very own feasts, where they dance, as it were, in spite of the tourists. Whoever has witnessed it will never forget it. On our travels abroad we often came across the same deep sincerity expressed in the dance, but always, without exception, it was far away from the big cities, in places where the people had kept their traditions, whether in mountain villages of the Alps, in small towns in the Balkans, in the plains of Argentina. . . .

In the United States, too, there is a marked revival of interest in genuine old folk dances. Although America is spoken of as a "new country," everything American once came from an old country. It would be most interesting and rewarding if every family would search earnestly for the folk dances of its own people, its ancestors. Much research has been done recently, and many good books, many records are now available. Let us think of the wonderful entertainment at a parish party if people were asked to contribute a folk dance from the country where their family came from. Of course, in the national costume! And this should not be taken lightly. I see no other way to protect our young people from the frequently pernicious influence of modern ballroom dancing. There is no use in just talking against it; something better has to be substituted. Here I speak from experience, as this is what we have done in our Music Camp in the summer for ten years. I also know from experience that it is very difficult to learn folk dancing from a printed description. Everyone should treat himself to a course, of which there are many new ones starting every year. Simply to get into the spirit, the atmosphere, into the very idea of folk dancing is something we should not miss, and then we have to pass on what we have found.

Carnival would be *the* time of the year to launch out on a program of folk dancing. Let me add that folk dancing and square dancing are not identical. Square dancing is only one group of folk dances coming from the British Isles. Many people think this is all there is to folk dancing, and since square dances are rather fast and exhausting, they say, "This is only for kids—I'm too old for that!" But there are dozens and dozens of quiet, beautiful, sometimes simple, sometimes intricate dances of the different nations. And let us also consider this: While we cannot learn dozens of foreign languages, we still can learn to understand the self-expression of nations in their music and in their folk dances. So why not make a firm plan for the coming Carnival season? For instance, to spend three evenings of every week in learning new folk dances. On Sunday afternoon, there might be a real party, either in the homes of different families in turn, or in a parish hall.

On other evenings we might have fun at home by learning to play new games. Do we realize that there are hundreds, literally hundreds, of most entertaining games? We just do not know them. By inquiring among friends and by looking up books we should be able to add a few good ones to our repertoire every year during the weeks of Carnival. This is an indispensable store to draw from when there are parties to be arranged for family or other feasts during the rest of the year.

Let us put these weeks of Carnival to use and learn to dance together, play together, and sing together.

Yes, sing together! But not the superficial, mediocre hits of the juke boxes, short-lived like the fly; let us rather make it our business to find gay songs among the good old folksongs. Some of those we have heard Burl Ives sing; there are also one or the other gay Negro spirituals—let us endeavor to add at least one good, worthwhile, gay song every week of Carnival so that we have something to contribute when we meet the others on Sunday afternoon.

TURKEY IN THE STRAW

Called the most American of all tunes.

1. As I was go - in' down the road, a
3. Turkey in the hay, tur-key in the straw, the
4. Well I met Mister Cat-fish come down the stream, says

Tur- key in the straw, tur-key in the hay,

1. tir - ed team an' a heav - y load, I
3. old gray mare won't gee nor haw, roll 'em
4. Mis - ter Cat -fish what does you mean? I

tur - key in the straw, tur - key in the hay,

THE ECHO YODEL

From the Austrian Alps.

THE RIDDLE SONG

Folksong from the Kentucky Mountains. In England known since the 15th century.

2. How can there be a cherry that has no stone?
   How can there be a chicken that has no bone?
   How can there be a ring that has no end?
   How can there be a baby with no cryin'?

3. A cherry, when it's blooming, it has no stone.
   A chicken when it's pipping, it has no bone.
   A ring when it's rolling, it has no end,
   A baby when it's sleeping, has no cryin'.

AUNT RHODY

"A song that is completely American in origin" (Burl Ives).

Go tell Aunt Rho-dy, go tell Aunt Rho - dy,

Go tell Aunt Rho - dy, go tell Aunt Rho - dy,

go tell Aunt Rho - dy that her old gray goose is

go tell Aunt Rho — dy that her old gray goose is

dead. The one that she's been a - sav - in,' the

dead. The one that she's been a - sav - in,' the

one that she's been a - sav - in,' the one that she's been a-

one that she's been a - sav - in,' the one that she's been a-

sav - in,' to make a feath-er - bed. She

sav - in,' to make a feath-er - bed. She

died in the mill - pond, she died in the mill - pond, she

died in the mill - pond, she died in the mill - pond, she

died in the mill-pond standin' on her head. The

died in the mill - pond standin' on her head. The

gos - lings are cryin', the gos - lings are cry - in', the

gos - lings are cry - in', the gos - lings are cry - in', the

gos– lings are cry–in', 'cause their mammy's dead.

gos – lings are cry – in', 'cause their mam–my's dead.

Go tell Aunt Rho – dy, go tell Aunt Rho – dy,

Go tell Aunt Rho – dy, go tell Aunt Rho – dy,

go tell Aunt Rho–dy that her old gray goose is dead.

go tell Aunt Rho – dy that her old gray goose is dead.

Spent like this the weeks of Carnival seem to fly. Every day the family is eagerly looking forward to the evening's program, whether it be singing or folk dancing or playing games or masquerading.

One more feature of Carnival time is the food and drink, the specialties of the season. To understand the special character of Carnival pastry—why it is always fried in deep fat, why it is full of eggs and milk and meat—we have to go back to the beginning when Lent was really the time of fast and abstinence, when it was forbidden not only to eat meat, but also milk and cream and everything made thereof, such as butter and cheese. The closer Ash Wednesday came, the more housewives tried to clear the kitchen and pantry of the forbidden goods. As these included any kind of lard and fat, they were used in these last days to make those delicious *Faschingskrapfen*, a kind of glorified jelly doughnut.

Faschingskrapfen

2 cups milk	1½ cup sugar
1 cake yeast	4 eggs
½ cup water	¼ cup lard
6 cups flour	1 tsp. salt

Scald the milk and allow to cool. Dissolve the yeast in the water, which should be warm. Add ½ cup flour. Mix thoroughly. Add this to the milk with a little of the sugar. Then add 3 cups flour, sifted. Let rise, preferably overnight. Beat the eggs well and add the lard and the rest of the sugar. Mix well. Stir in enough of the remaining flour to make a stiff dough. Let it rise again. Turn out on a floured pastry board and roll to ¼-inch thickness. Cut out and let the doughnuts rise to double their bulk. Fill them with apricot jam. Then fry in deep fat at 360 degrees three to four minutes, turning as they fry. Drain on absorbent paper.

The last three days before Ash Wednesday everywhere, not only in Austria, but also in other countries, pancakes (*Palatschinken* in Austria) were eaten, obviously merely because eggs and butter and milk had to be finished off before the fasting began, and pancakes took care of a great many eggs and much milk and butter! These last days before Ash Wednesday are the climax of Carnival. In the Catholic countries, where Lent afterwards would be taken seriously, work was stopped. People made merry practically day and night. In South America it still seems to be this way, according to stories we have heard in Rio! The last day of Carnival is *"Mardi Gras"* or *"Faschingsdienstag"* or "Fat Tuesday." This should be a big celebration, if possible of the whole parish together, or a circle of friends, and everything which one did during the previous weeks should be done just once more. "Once more this dance!" "Once more this song!" "Once more this game!"—until twelve o'clock sharp. When the clock strikes twelve, in the middle of the dance, according to the good old tradition, one should stop and the whole group should kneel down and say one "Our Father" together and then, rising up, say, "I wish you a blessed season of Lent" and go home.

It has to be experienced to be fully believed, but there is a great blessing on such a Carnival time, shared in a family. To have spent a good Carnival will finally prove to the greater honor and glory of God, in enabling us to spend a good Lent!

Easter Cycle

Pre-Lent

SEPTUAGESIMA TO ASH WEDNESDAY

WITH Septuagesima Sunday begins the cycle that has for its center the greatest of all solemnities, the feast of Easter. The Christmas cycle and the Easter cycle are like the water and wine at the Offertory when the priest prays: "Grant that by the mystery of this water and wine we may be made partakers of His Divinity, Who vouchsafed to become partaker of our humanity, Jesus Christ Thy Son, Our Lord." For in the Christmas cycle we celebrate God having come down among us, clothing Himself with our humanity. This is the cycle of the Incarnation, corresponding to the cycle of the Redemption where we are shown this same Jesus Who "makes us partakers of His Divinity."

These two and a half weeks—the Septuagesima, Sexuagesima, and Quinquagesima Sundays, and the Monday, Tuesday, and Wednesday following Quinquagesima—serve as a time of transition for the soul, which must pass from Christmas joys (and through the merry time of Carnival) to the stern penance of the sacred forty days of Lent. The fast is not yet an obligation, but the color of the vestments is already violet. The Gloria during Holy Mass is suspended, and the martyrology introduces Septuagesima Sunday as that Sunday on which "we lay aside the song of the Lord which is Alleluia." In medieval times they used to "bury the Alleluia" solemnly in the cathedral and in the abbey churches. This custom was nearly forgotten, but we came across it again on the happy day when we were

101

privileged to celebrate Holy Mass in the creative and inspired parish of our friend, Monsignor Martin Hellriegel. There, in a solemn procession, the school children carried a wooden tablet on which was engraved the word "Alleluia" through the main aisle of the church over to the altar of the Blessed Mother where they put it at her feet and covered it with a purple cloth. There it would remain until Easter, when, in a triumphant tone of voice, the priest would intone, for the first time after forty days, a three-fold Alleluia.

This impressed us so deeply that we wished it could be introduced into all parish churches, to make the congregation conscious that Alleluia is the ancient Hebrew chant of triumph with which a victor was hailed after the battle. It is also the chant St. John heard in heaven, as he tells us in the Apocalypse. This Alleluia has to be suspended in a time devoted to fathoming the thought that we are "poor, banished children of Eve, mourning and weeping in this valley of tears." Only in the Easter festivities shall we again hail Our Lord, the victor over Satan, Who will reopen to us the kingdom of heaven.

In these weeks of the pre-Lenten season, the mother of the family has much to teach her children. She will introduce them to the meaning of the color of violet in church. She will prepare them for the forty sacred days of retreat, and will help them to formulate their Lenten resolutions, which should be written on a sheet of paper and placed on the house altar. It is important that Lenten resolutions do not use the negative approach only, such as, "I won't do this" and "I won't do that." They should start positively, with "I will use these three books" (this as soon as the child can read) ; "I will use the time I save by abstaining from television for this and this. . . ." "I will use the money I save by not going to the movies for alms given to. . . ."

It is a precious time, a time for the mother to introduce her children to the three ancient good works—prayer, fasting, and giving of alms—with which we can atone for our sins. It will take root in young hearts, never to be forgotten.

ANTIPHON FOR LENT

Fifth (Lydian) mode. Recite the Psalm "Miserere" (Psalm 50), repeating the Antiphon after every four or five verses of the psalm, and at the end.

In - cline Thine ear, O Lord, and show us mer - cy, for we are sin - ners be - fore Thee.

Lent

L ENT is primarily known as a time devoted to fast and abstinence. Our non-Catholic friends feel sorry for us because we have to watch our food. "Isn't it an awful strain?"

But this is only one side of the season of Lent, and not even the most important one. First and foremost, these weeks between Ash Wednesday and Holy Saturday are set aside as a time of preparation for the greatest feast of the year, Easter.

We are not fasting in commemoration of Our Lord's fast of forty days, but are imitating Him in his fast of preparation—preparation for His great work of Redemption. It is the same with us. Once a year we take forty days out of the three hundred and sixty-five, and we too fast in preparation: in preparation for the commemoration of our Redemption.

We all should get together and work toward the restoration of the meaning of Lent. People nowadays see in it just a gloomy time full of "must nots." That is a great pity, because Lent is a solemn season rich in hidden mysteries. We must also keep in mind that Lent is only a part of the great Easter season, that it is for Easter what Advent was for Christmas, and that Lent taken by itself would make no more sense than Advent without Christmas at its end. Therefore, we should let Holy Mother Church take us by the hand and lead us— not each soul alone, but the whole family as a group—away from the noise of the world into a forty-day retreat.

No other time of the year has been so singled out by the Church as this, in that a completely different Mass is provided for every single day, beginning with Ash Wednesday and continuing through the octave day of Easter; and again for the crowning feast of the Easter season, the eight days of Pentecost. If we keep the closed time as faithfully as our forefathers did—which means keeping away from all noisy outside entertainment such as cocktail parties and dances—then we shall find ample time for the imitation of Christ as it is outlined in every morning's Mass.

The restoration of the season of Lent was begun in the year when the Holy Father gave back to us the Easter Night. As we now know that in this holiest of all nights we shall be permitted to be reborn in Christ, renewing solemnly, with a lighted candle in our hands, our baptismal vows, we understand more and more clearly the two great thoughts which the Church is developing throughout the whole of Lent: the instruction of the catechumens and the deepening of the contrition of the penitents. Instruction and penance shall become our motto also for these holy weeks.

Instruction—this brings us to the Lenten reading program. The time saved through abstention from movies—and it is astonishing to find how much it is!—will be devoted to a carefully chosen reading program. Every year we should divide our reading into three parts: something for the mind, something for the heart, something for the soul.

Something for the mind: This should mean doing serious research. One year we might work on the history of the Church; another year on the sacraments; or we might carefully study a scholarly life of Our Lord Jesus Christ; or a book on Christian ethics; or the Encyclicals of the Pope; or a book on dogma.

For the soul: This should be spiritual reading of a high order, from the works of the saints or saintly writers. For example, *The Ascent of Mt. Carmel*, by St. John of the Cross; *The Introduction to a Devout Life*, by St. Francis de Sales; *The Story of a Soul*, by St. Thérèse of Lisieux; *The Spiritual Castle*, by St. Teresa of Avila; *The Soul of the Apostolate*, by Abbot Chautard; the books of Abbot Marmion, and similar works.

For the heart: According to the old proverb, "*Exempla trahunt*," it is most encouraging to read the biographies of people who started out as we did but had their minds set on following the word of Our Lord, "Be you therefore perfect, as also your heavenly Father is perfect." In other words, to read a well-written biography of a saint (canonized or not) will have the same effect on us as it had once on St. Augustine, who said, after watching saintly people living a holy life: "If he could do it, and she, why not I?" But it has to be a well-written biography, that is, a book showing a human being in the round, with all his shortcomings that had to be overcome by faithful cooperation with grace—and not the old-fashioned hagiography in sugar-candy style with its doubtful statements, carefully stressing that the saint is born a full-fledged saint by describing how the holy baby refused his mother's breast every Saturday in honor of the Blessed Mother (and, of course, the first words of these remarkable beings invariably must be a piously lisped "Jesus and Mary"). These "saints" never made a mistake, never succumbed to temptation—in other words, their literary portraits are identical replicas of their statues in the show windows in Barclay Street and just as inspiring. But we are lucky: the worst seems to be behind us. A new school of writing of the lives of the saints has begun.

If every member of a family adopts this threefold reading program and comments on the books he has been working on, a great benefit will be flowing from one to the other as they exchange the spiritual goods obtained from their reading. I remember how the enthusiasm of each reader made us exchange books after Lent was over. Years ago it began with the books of Henry Ghéon: first, *The Secret of the Little Flower*, followed by the other secrets of the saints. Another year it was *The History of a Family*, with its background story of the most irresistible saint of our days, Thérèse of Lisieux. Recently we all found *St. Teresa of Avila,* by Marcelle Auclair, the best and most readable of all biographies of this great saint. After we had seen the great film, *Monsieur Vincent,* we were naturally interested in reading Monsignor Jean Calvet's version of the saint's life, *St. Vincent de Paul.*

There is no saying how much such an extensive reading program adds to the richness of family life, how many new topics are introduced, to be talked about during the family meals. And one book that should certainly be read aloud during these days of the great retreat is the Holy Bible. It would be a good idea to lean, for one year at least, close to the selections the Church herself makes in the breviary of the priests. In another year one could take one of the prophets (Isaias during Advent, Jeremias during Lent), and go on from there until every book of Holy Scriptures has been read aloud and discussed in the family. In this way we have read through the books of the Old and New Testaments more than once, and have found them an unending source of happiness and spiritual growth. Any family that has tried it will never want to give it up. To set aside the "closed times" of the year for daily reading aloud is one of the most profitable uses of the time gained. As many questions will be asked, it will be necessary to obtain some source in which to find at least some of the answers. A commentary on the Holy Scriptures should be in every Christian house.

If the first thought recurring through the liturgy of Lent is instruction, the second is penance. To understand better what was originally meant by that word, let us go back to the beginning when the Church was young and the zeal and fervor unbroken. Father Weiser, in his *Easter Book,* tells us about it:

> Persons who had committed serious public sin and scandal were enjoined on Ash Wednesday with the practice of "public penance." The period of the penance lasted until Holy Thursday when they were solemnly reconciled, absolved from their sins, and allowed to receive Holy Communion. . . . The imposition of public penance on Ash Wednesday was an official rite in Rome as early as the fourth century; and soon spread to all Christianized nations. Numerous descriptions of this ancient ceremony have been preserved in medieval manuscripts and, in every detail, breathe

a spirit of harshness and humility really frightening to us of the present generation.

Public sinners approached their priests shortly before Lent to accuse themselves of their misdeeds and were presented by the priests on Ash Wednesday to the bishop of the place. Outside the cathedral, poor and noble alike stood barefoot, dressed in sackcloth, heads bowed in humble contrition. The bishop, assisted by his canons, assigned to each one particular acts of penance according to the nature and gravity of his crime. Whereupon they entered the church, the bishop leading one of them by the hand, the others following in single file, holding each other's hands. Before the altar, not only the penitents, but also the bishop and all his clergy recited the seven penitential psalms. [Psalms 6, 31, 37, 50, 101, 129, 142.] Then, as each sinner approached, the bishop imposed his hands on him, sprinkled him with holy water, threw the blessed ashes on his head, and invested him with the hair shirt. Finally he admonished ("with tears and sighs" as the regulation suggests) : "Behold you are cast out from the sight of holy mother Church because of your sins and crimes, as Adam the first man was cast out of Paradise because of his transgression." After this ceremony the penitents were led out of the church and forbidden to re-enter until Holy Thursday (for the solemn rite of their reconciliation). Meanwhile they would spend Lent apart from their families in a monastery or some other place of voluntary confinement, where they occupied themselves with prayer, manual labor, and works of charity. Among other things they had to go barefoot all through Lent, were forbidden to converse with others, were made to sleep on the ground or on a bedding of straw, and were unable to bathe or cut their hair.

Such was the public penance (in addition to the general Lenten fast) for "ordinary" cases of great sin and scandal. . . . For especially shocking and heinous crimes a much longer term was imposed. An ancient manuscript records the case of an English nobleman of the eleventh century who received a penance of seven years for notorious crimes and scandals committed. The duties of his first year of public penance consisted of the following details : he must not bear arms (a bitter humiliation for a nobleman of that time!); he must not receive Holy Communion except in danger of death; he must not enter the church to attend Mass but remain standing outside the church door; he must eat very sparingly, taking meat only on Sundays and major feasts; on three days of the week he must abstain from wine; he must feed one poor person every day from what he would have spent on himself. The document closes with the words: "If, however, thou shalt have borne this penance willingly for one year, in the future, with God's grace, thou shalt be judged more leniently."*

And Father Weiser adds a helpful remark. "These examples will make clear, perhaps, what an indulgence granted by the Church means in our time. An indulgence of seven years is the remission of temporal punishment for sins already forgiven to the extent of a seven years' personal penance such as just described."

After having seen what penance meant to our fathers in the faith, it will be interesting to see how much of it is still alive in our times.

The first day of Lent is Ash Wednesday. As we are summoned into church we find the program all laid out for us. Following the example of the people of Nineveh, who did penance in sackcloth and ashes, the Church wants today to humble our pride by reminding us of our death sentence as a consequence of our sins. She sprinkles our head with ashes and says: "Remember, man, that thou art dust, and unto dust shalt thou return." The ashes used have been made from burning the palm from the previous Palm Sunday. These ashes belong to the very powerful sacramentals (such as Epiphany water or candles from Candlemas Day). The four prayers preceding the blessing of the ashes are so beautiful and so rich in meaning that they should be read aloud and discussed in the family circle on Ash Wednesday night.

In our time, when "how to" books are so popular, the Gospel seems most appropriate to instruct us on how to fast: "At that time Jesus said to His disciples, 'When you fast, be ye not as hypocrites, sad, for they disfigure their faces that they may appear unto men to fast. Amen, I say to you, they have received their reward, but thou, when thou fastest, anoint thy head and wash thy face that thou appear not to men to fast but to thy Father Who sees in secret, and thy Father, Who sees in secret, will repay thee.' " It is interesting to

* Francis X. Weiser, *The Easter Book*, pp. 46 f. New York, Harcourt, Brace & Co., 1954.

remind ourselves that fast and abstinence are such ancient practices that they are much older than the Catholic Church, as are ashes and haircloth as means of penance. The pages of the Old Testament are filled with references to sackcloth and ashes (Jonas 3:5-8; Jeremias 6:26; 25:34; Judith 9:1).

The ancient notions about fast and abstinence compare to our modern Lenten regulations as a Roman chariot compares to a modern sports car. Let us, first of all, straighten out what is fasting and what is abstinence. The first has to do with the quantity of food that can be taken, and the latter refers to the kind of food. In ancient times fasting really was fasting. The first meal was taken after vespers, and vespers were sung at sundown as evening prayer of the Church. Abstinence in the old times (and the old times reached almost to the days of our grandparents) meant that nothing was eaten (or kept in the house) which comes from animals: no meat, no fish, no lard, no milk, butter, cheese, cream. The Lenten fare consisted exclusively of vegetables, fruit, and a bread made of flour and water and salt. For our generation the law of abstinence means that all meat of warm-blooded animals and of birds and fowl and the soup made thereof is forbidden. It leaves free the wonderful world of seafood and the meat of other cold-blooded animals such as frogs, turtles, snails, etc.

The fast means that we are allowed one full meal every day and two other meals which, if put together, do not exceed in quantity the full meal.

When I inquired once why the law of fast and abstinence is so much more lenient for us than it was for previous generations, I was told that modern man is much too frail to undergo the awful rigors of the ancient practice. After all, have we not experienced two world wars in our generation which have weakened our constitutions? That seemed to make perfect sense to me until just recently. I got infected by a neighbor of ours in Stowe with the popular preoccupation of which is the best diet. Together we searched through a library of books, one more interesting than the other, the sum total of all them most confusing and astounding, however. Among other things I learned that almost all the ancient and modern sages of the science of "how to live longer and look younger" (they all boast of a tradition going back into the gray dawn of time with the yogis of India) agree on several points: (1) We are all over-eating— we should eat much less. (2) We are all eating too much meat, which sours our system, and we absolutely have to abstain from meat for longer or shorter periods every year. (3) If we could adapt ourselves to a diet of raw vegetables and fruit and whole-wheat bread, that would be the ideal. (4) And now I could hardly believe my eyes when I read, not once, but in several places, that it would do simply miracles for our constitution if we only would let ourselves be persuaded to undergo a period of complete fast. (One authority suggests three days, others a week, ten days, up to thirty, forty, and even sixty days!)

I cannot help but think sadly: Woe if the Church ever had dared to make such a law or even give only a slight hint in the direction of undergoing a complete fast—for the love of God! Obviously, modern man, after all, is not too frail to undergo the awful rigors of ancient fast and abstinence. The constitution of man seems not to have changed at all, then. What has changed are the motives. While the early Christians abstained from food and drink and meat and eggs out of a great sense of sorrow for their sins, and for love of God took upon themselves these inconveniences, modern man has as motive the "body beautiful," the "girlish figure," the "how to look younger and live longer" motive. These selfish motives are strong enough to convince him that fasting is good for him—in fact, it is fun.

We ought to be grateful to these modern apostles, whether from India, Switzerland, Sweden, or Wisconsin, because their teaching shows that Holy Mother Church is equally interested in the spiritual welfare of her children and in their physical health. It also should make us better Christians. It should be absolutely unbearable to us to think that there are thousands of people around us who pride themselves on rigorous feats of fast and abstinence for motives as flimsy as good looks, while we cannot bring ourselves to give up a bare minimum. And so it might not be a bad idea after all, in fact a very modern one, to go back to the practice of former days and clear our house during the last day of Carnival of every trace of meat and butter and eggs, fish and lard and bouillon cubes, and spend six wholesome weeks in complete harmony with the health-food store around the corner: eating fresh fruit salads, drinking carrot juice, revelling in the exceeding richness of the vitamins we find in raw celery, fresh spinach, and pumpernickel. I have repeatedly read now that there is absolutely nothing to it to undergo a complete fast. One can even continue one's occupation, and afterwards (the afterwards can be after thirty days, I was assured) one feels newly born and twenty years younger. All right, if this is so, let us not be so soft any more. What can be done "to feel twenty years younger" must be possible for our own reason: "that our fasts may be pleasing to Thee, O Lord, and a powerful remedy." (Post Communion, Ash Wednesday).

Today we do eat too much—we eat too many things at one meal; we eat much too much meat; we consume an unhealthy amount of strong liquor and too much coffee and tea, which are bad for our nerves; and (this is perhaps our deepest conviction) the bread we can buy in stores is not the daily bread we pray for in the "Our Father," but something on the line of soft, tender sponge rubber, white sponge rubber. It has made us return to the dark rye bread, the home-made rye bread we used to have in Austria. All our guests rave about it, and so we want to share our recipe with others.

Dark Rye Bread

4 cups medium rye flour	½ tsp. caraway seed
2 cups regular white flour	1 cake yeast, or 1 package dry
1 tbsp. salt	yeast
	4 cups warm water

Dissolve yeast in 1 cup warm water until it starts to rise and make bubbles. Pour this on the flour. Add three more cups of warm water to the flour and stir until fluid is all soaked up. Then knead (with your own hands) until it is a firm, fairly stiff dough. Put in warm place to rise, covering it with a cloth. After two hours or more (depending on temperature of the room), the dough should rise to twice the size. Punch it down and knead for about 10 minutes again. Cover it up and let it rise again until not quite double the size. It will rise in a short while (½ hour to ¾ hour). Heat oven to 350 degrees F. Then put dough upside down on a flour-sprinkled cookie sheet. Make holes in the dough with a knitting needle (or something similar) while in the hot stove. Leave there for an hour, then "wash" the bread: take it half way out and brush it freely with water. Push back into oven for another quarter hour, turning heat down to 300 degrees F. Then take it out. Makes 1 loaf.

And here we should not forget that the pretzel, which is now quite popular at our parties, goes back to the early times when only bread made of flour and water, with a little salt, was allowed during Lent. In order to make it a little more appealing, it was first shaped in the form of a ring and a cross in memory of the Cross of Our Lord, and later it took on the present-day shape of two arms crossed in prayer. It is said to have been used in the monastery schools of the medieval abbeys as a prize for the pupils and that the name comes from the Latin word *pretiolum*. In Austria, southern Germany, and Poland, on St. Joseph's Day, March 19th, a man would go around and sell pretzels on the streets and the people would eat them for lunch, together with a "Josephi beer," a special dark, very malted beer.

In the middle of Lent comes the Sunday Laetare, also called "Rose Sunday." It is as if Holy Mother Church wants to give us a break by interrupting the solemn chant of mourning, the unaccompanied cadences and the use of the violet vestments, bursting out suddenly in the word *"Laetare"* ("Rejoice"), allowing her priests to vest in rose-colored garments, to have flowers on the altar and an organ accompaniment for chant. It is also called "Rose Sunday" because on that day the Pope in Rome blesses a golden rose, an ornament made of gold and precious stones. The Holy Father prays that the Church may bring forth the fruit of good works and "the perfume of the ointment of the flowers from the root of Jesse." Then he sends the golden rose to some church or city in the world or to a person who has been of great service to the Church.

Only recently I discovered that this Sunday used to be known as "Mothering Sunday." This seems to go back to an ancient custom. People in every city would visit the cathedral, or mother church, inspired by a reference in the Epistle read on the Fourth Sunday of Lent: "That Jerusalem which is above, is free, which is our Mother." And there grew up, first in England, from where it spread over the continent, the idea that children who did not live at home visited their mothers that day and brought them a gift. This is, in fact, the precursor of our Mother's Day. Expecting their visiting children, the mothers are said to have baked a special cake in which they used equal amounts of sugar and flour (two cups of each); from this came the name "Simmel Cake," derived from the Latin word *similis,* meaning "like" or "same." Here is the recipe:

Simmel Cake

¾ cup butter
2 cups sugar
2 cups flour
4 eggs

⅓ cup shredded lemon & orange peel
1 cup currants
almond paste
½ tsp. salt.

Cream the butter and sugar until smooth. Add the eggs one at a time, beating after each addition. Sift the flour and salt and add to the first mixture. Dust the peel and currants with a little flour and add to the batter. Line cake tin with waxed paper and pour in half the dough. Add a layer of almond paste and remaining dough. Bake at 300 degrees F. for one hour. Ice with a thin white icing, flavored with a few drops of almond extract.

And every evening in Lent, we sing a Lenten hymn—two of our favorite ones are given here.

O HEAD ALL SCARRED AND BLEEDING

Original melody by Hans Lee Hassler, 1601. Used in this form
by J. S. Bach in the *St. Matthew Passion.* Translation, Henry S.
Drinker.

O Head all scarred and bleed - ing, and heaped with cru-el
scorn! O Head so filled with sor - row, and
bound with crown of thorn! O Head that was so
hon - ored, so love-ly fair to see, and
now so low de - grad - ed! My heart goes out to Thee.

2. *Thou countenance so noble,*
Yet now so pale and wan,
Which all the world should honor,
Now foully spat upon.
No more Thine eyes are shining,
That once did shine so bright;
Ill-usage and maligning,
Affliction, shame and spite.

OPEN, O HARD AND SINFUL HEART!

Text, Angelus Silesius, 1637; melody, 1638.

O - pen, oh hard and sin - ful heart,
Think of His pain and bit - ter part,

God will re - turn to heed you.
Let not more guilt im - pede you.

He who to pe - nance is in - spired,

Shall then in truth be li - ving.

The sin - ner's death God ne'er de - sired,

His mer - cy is for - giv - ving.

2. Open your eyes, believe, be wise,
   With God there's no pretending.
   Your sorry soul in danger lies
   Of death and pains unending.
   Come back, come back, O wayward one.
   Shake off the sins that bind you.
   Surely God's own almighty Throne
   Plentiful grace will find you.

3. Open your heart, your God behold,
   With outstretched hands so tender,
   On the dread cross in grief untold
   His life for you surrender.
   A trembling rends the hardest stone,
   Sun, moon and stars are darkened.
   Are you unsoftened, you alone,
   Have you to Him not harkened?

Passiontide

THE LITURGY follows Christ's early life step by step. At Christmas season we learn of the birth in the stable, the adoration of the shepherds, the slaughter of the innocents, the flight into Egypt, the adoration of the Magi, and finally the return from Egypt. Then we meet Our Lord again at His baptism, we accompany Him into the desert on his fast, and we go with Him for the first and second years of His public life, we listen to His parables, we admire His miracles, and we unite our hearts with Him in His life of toil and missionary love for us.

Now four weeks of instruction have passed. We have followed Our Lord in His apostolic ministry and we have reached the moment when, together with Holy Mother Church, we shall contemplate the sorrowful happenings of the last year (during Passion Week) and the last week (during Holy Week) of His life on earth. We can feel the hatred of Christ's enemies growing day by day. On Good Friday we shall witness once more the most frightening of all happenings, foretold by the prophets and even by Our Lord Himself, the bloody drama of Calvary.

The purpose of Passiontide is to call to our memory the persecutions of which Our Lord was the object during His public life and especially toward the end. If Septuagesima season acts as a remote preparation for Easter, and Lent the proximate one, the last two weeks of Passiontide are the immediate preparation.

PASSION SUNDAY

When the children were still very small, I said to them on the way to church on a Passion Sunday morning, "Now watch and tell me what is different today in church!" On the way home they said eagerly that the statues and crosses on the altars were covered with violet cloth.

"And why don't we do it at home, Mother? Shouldn't we cover the crucifix and statues in the living room and in our bedrooms, too?"

As I had no good reason to offer against it, we bought a few yards of violet cloth the next day and did at home what we had seen in church. In the following years we were ready for the covering ceremony on Saturday before Passion Sunday.

The older ones among the children also had noticed that the prayers at the foot of the altar were much shorter and that there was no *Gloria Patri* after the Introit and the Lavabo. To let the children watch for such changes in the liturgy makes them much more eager than if they are told everything in advance. Promptly, when we came in our evening prayers to the *Gloria Patri*, a warning, hissing "Sssh" from the children's side made us aware that *Gloria Patri*, even if only in family prayers, should be omitted for these holy days of mourning.

I am sure it would be the case in every family, as it was in ours, that the children are the ones who most eagerly want to carry into the home as much of holy liturgy as they possibly can. For instance, when I answered their question as to how the ashes are obtained which are to be blessed on Ash Wednesday, telling them that the blessed palms from the previous Palm Sunday are burned, they asked a most logical question: "But, Mother, if you burn a blessed object, aren't the ashes already blessed? And if so, shouldn't we burn all the blessed palms around the place too and sprinkle the ashes over the garden?" And so we did! After we had established this as a firm family custom, I read that this is done in many places in the Austrian Alps, only there the people strew the ashes not over the garden, but over the fields.

PALM SUNDAY

Then comes the week which is called in the missal "Hebdomada Major"—our "Holy Week" in which we accompany Our Lord day by day through the last week of His life, as it is told in the Gospels. First we join Him in His triumphant entry into Jerusalem on Palm Sunday.

As soon as the Church had been freed by the Emperor Constantine in the fourth century, the Christians began to celebrate Palm Sunday in a very dramatic way in Jerusalem. On the very spot where it had happened, the holy texts were read: "Rejoice, daughter of Sion, behold Thy King will come to thee. . . ." The crowd spread their garments on the ground, crying aloud, "Blessed be the King Who cometh in the Name of the Lord." The bishop, mounted on an ass, would ride up to the church on the Mount of Olives, surrounded by a multitude carrying palms and singing hymns and joyful anthems.

From Jerusalem this re-enactment of Christ's solemn entry into His holy city came to Rome, where the Church soon adopted the same practice. The ceremony, however, was preceded by the solemn reading of the passage from Holy Scriptures relating the flight from Egypt, thus reminding Christ's people that Christ, the new Moses, in giving them the real manna, is delivering them out of the Egypt of sin and nourishing them in the Eucharist.

Around the ninth century the Church added a new rite. The palms, which the people would hold in their hands when they accompanied their bishop, were solemnly blessed. We have already witnessed several of these specially solemn blessings, on Epiphany, on Candlemas Day, on Ash Wednesday. Again these texts are so rich in beautiful thoughts for meditation that families should read them together—not only read them, but read them prayerfully.

From Rome the idea to re-enact Our Lord's triumphal entry into Jerusalem spread all over the Christian world. In medieval times the faithful and the clergy met at a chapel or a wayside shrine outside of town where the palms were blessed, and from there moved in a solemn procession to the cathedral. Our Lord was represented either by the bishop riding on an ass or, in some places, by the Blessed

Sacrament carried by the king or, in other places, by a crucifix carried ahead. In some Austrian villages the figure of Christ sitting on an ass, carved in wood, is carried.

The Christian people had an unerring instinct for the efficacy of those solemnly blessed sacramentals, and just as they carried home Epiphany water and holy candles, they also would bring home with them blessed palms. In the old country this was quite an elaborate function of "the liturgy in the home." As we did not have real palms growing in Austria, we used evergreens and pussy willows, which at that time were the first children of spring. Like all other Austrian families living in the country, we made as many little bouquets as there were divisions on our grounds—one for the vegetable garden, one for the orchard, one for the flower garden, one for each pasture, and one for each field. Each of these little bouquets was fastened to a stick about three feet high. Besides, there were many single twigs of pussy willow which would be placed behind pictures all around the house. These bouquets were gaily adorned with colored ribbons or dyed shavings from the carpenter shop. The children carried them into the church and vied with each other, during the blessing, as to who held his stick highest to get most of the holy water sprinkled on it. Then bouquets were carried in a liturgical procession and afterwards were brought home. In the afternoon the whole family would follow the father throughout the house and all over the grounds and he would place in the middle of every lot one of those sticks carrying the blessed bouquets as a means of protecting his property against the influence of evil spirits, against the damage of hail storms and floods. While the family would proceed from lot to lot, they would say the rosary. We would alternate between decades of the rosary and the chants of the day, *Pueri Hebraeorum* and *Gloria, laus et honor*. On Easter Sunday the family would revisit these sticks, bringing along little bottles filled with Easter water (holy water blessed solemnly on Easter morning). These little bottles would be tied to sticks, thus adding another sacramental.

HOLY WEEK

According to an old tradition, the first three days of Holy Week—Monday, Tuesday, Wednesday—are dedicated to spring cleaning. In the days before the invention of the vacuum cleaner, this was a spectacular undertaking: sofas, easy chairs, and all mattresses would be carried out of the house and beaten mercilessly with a *Teppich-pracker* (carpet-beater). Walls were dusted, curtains were changed —a thorough domestic upheaval. There is little time for cooking, and meals are made of leftovers.

By Wednesday night the house looks spick and span. And now the great *Feierabend* begins. *Feierabend* is an untranslatable word. It really means vigil—evening before a feast, the evening before Sunday, when work ceases earlier than on any other weekday in order to allow time to get into the mood to celebrate. *Feier* means "to celebrate," *Abend* means "evening." From now on until the Tuesday after Easter no unnecessary work will be done on our place. These days are set aside for Our Lord. On Wednesday, with all the satisfaction of having set our house at peace, and after the dishes of a simple early supper are finished, we go down to the village church in Stowe for the first Tenebrae service. In the sanctuary, a large wrought-iron triangular candlestick is put up, with fifteen dark candles. We take our places in the choir, and the solemn chanting of matins and lauds begins. This is the first part of the Divine Office, which has been recited daily around the world by all priests and many religious since the early times of the Church. In the cathedrals and many monasteries it is chanted in common. For the last days of Holy Week, it is performed in public, so to speak—not only in cathedral churches, but in any church, so that the faithful may take part in it.

We always consider this the greatest honor for us, the singing family, the greatest reward for all the trouble that goes along with life in public, that we can sing for all the Divine Offices in church.

Matins has three nocturnes, each one consisting of three psalms with their antiphons and three lessons. The first nocturne is always the most solemn one. We sing all the psalms on their respective *tonus*. We sing the antiphons, some in Gregorian chant, some from the compositions of the old masters such as Palestrina, Lassus, Vittorio.

The lessons were sung last year by Father Wasner, Werner, and Johannes. In the second and third nocturne we only recite the psalms in *recto tono* in order not to make it too long. Some of the antiphons and all of the lessons, however, are sung. After each psalm the altar boy extinguishes a candle, reminding us of how one Apostle after the other left Our Lord. Matins is followed by lauds, consisting of five psalms and antiphons which we recite. At the end of lauds there is only one candle left—the symbol of Our Lord all by Himself crying out, "Where are you, O My people!" And we, in the name of all the people, recite now the *Miserere*, the famous penitential psalm, while the altar boy is carrying the last candle behind the altar and the church is now in complete darkness. At the end of the *Miserere* we all make a banging noise with the breviary books. This custom is quite ancient. It is supposed to indicate the earthquake at the moment of the Resurrection. After this noise, the altar boy emerges from behind the altar with the burning Christ-candle and puts it back on the candlestick. This is a ray of hope anticipating the glorious Easter night. (In Austria the Tenebrae service is called *Pumpernette,* or "noisy matins.")

The congregation is following closely with booklets in which the whole service, which we sing in Latin, is given in English. This is the most moving evening service of the whole year. When we sing *Tenebrae factae sunt,* an awesome silence falls upon the whole church, and when we sing the famous *Improperia "Popule meus"* by Palestrina we all are moved to the depths. Is there anything more heartrending than to listen to the outcry of the anxious Redeemer: "My people, what have I done to thee, or in what have I grieved thee, answer Me. What more ought I to do for thee that I have not done?"

On the morning of Holy Thursday, the Church in her service tries most movingly to combine the celebration of the two great events she wants to commemorate: "Who lives in memory of Him," Our Lord had said on the first Holy Thursday when He gave Himself to us in the Holy Eucharist; and, "Father, if it be possible, let this chalice pass from me. Nevertheless not as I will, but as thou wilt." This cry He uttered only a few hours later. Therefore, as the Solemn Mass begins, the festive strains of the organ accompany the chant of the Introit and Kyrie, and when the priest intones the Gloria, all the bells on the steeple, as well as in the church, ring together once more for the last time because, right afterwards, Holy Church, as the Bride of Christ, goes into mourning as she accompanies the Bridegroom through His hours of unspeakable suffering. The organ remains silent when she reminds the faithful in the Gradual: "Christ became obedient unto us to death, even unto the death of the Cross. . . ."

The Gospel of this day tells of the lesson Jesus gave us in brotherly love and humility as He first washed the feet of His disciples, afterwards saying: "Know you what I have done to you? You call me Master, and Lord; and you say well, for so I am. If then I being your Lord and Master, have washed your feet; you also ought to wash one another's feet. For I have given you an example, that as I have done to you, so you do also." Therefore, in all cathedrals and abbey churches the bishops and abbots go down on their knees on this day after Holy Mass and wash the feet of the twelve oldest members of their communities. It is wonderful that in our days more and more parishes are adopting this beautiful custom, which brings home to us better than the most eloquent sermon that we should remember this word of Our Lord: "For I have given you an example, that as I have done to you, so you do also," which should become increasingly the watchword in our daily life. This is what the Church wants us to take home with us on that day: the attitude of washing one another's feet; and, because we Catholics have not awakened to this fact, we are rightly to be blamed for all wrong and injustice and wars going on in the world!

As Good Friday has no Mass of its own, but only the "Mass of the Pre-Sanctified," an extra big host was consecrated by the priest during Mass on Holy Thursday, which is put into a chalice and covered up with a white cloth. This chalice is now incensed immediately after Mass and carried in solemn procession to the "Altar of Repose," while the *Pange Lingua* is chanted solemnly. This repository should remind us of the prison in which Our Lord was kept that terrible night from Thursday to Friday. Unlike that first night, where He was all alone after all the Apostles had fled, the faithful now take turns in keeping watch.

There is an old legend circulating in the old country, still fervently believed by the children, that all the bells fly to Rome on Holy Thursday, where the Holy Father blesses them; they return in time for the Gloria on Holy Saturday.

Another custom still alive in the villages throughout Austria is this: As the bell cannot be rung for the Angelus on these three days, the altar boys man their outdoor *Ratschen* (a kind of rattle looking like a toy wheelbarrow, whose one wheel grinds out deafening noise) and race through the streets, stopping at certain previously designated corners, lifting up their *Ratschen* and chanting in chorus:

> *Wir ratschen, ratschen zum englischen Gruss,*
> *Den jeder katholische Christ beten muss.*
> (We remind you by this noise of the Angelus,
> Of a prayer to be said by every faithful Christian.)

Needless to say, many a little boy's heart waits eagerly for these three holy days. While he might be too young to understand the great thoughts of Holy Week, he certainly is wide awake to his own responsibility of reminding his fellow-men, "Time to pray!"

My son Werner is living with his family just a little way down the road. When his little boys, Martin and Bernhard, are big enough to shoulder the responsibility, their father will make them such an old-world *Ratschen* and their mother will teach them the rhyme going with it.

In the house also, the bells have to be silent. The bell rung for the meals or for family devotions is replaced by a hand clapper worked by the youngest member of the family, who announces solemnly from door to door that lunch is ready.

Holy Thursday has a menu all its own. For the noon meal we have the traditional spring herb soup (*Siebenkraeutersuppe*).

Spring Herb Soup

Dandelions
Chervil
Cress
Sorrel
Leaf nettle

The mixture of the above herbs should total about 7 ounces. Whether bought at the market or picked, they should be washed well. Steam in butter with finely chopped onions and parsley. Press through a sieve into a flour soup and let it boil. You may put in one or two egg yolks, one to two tablespoons of cream, or ¼ cup milk. You also may use sour cream.

Afterwards there is the traditional spinach with fried eggs. In Austria, Holy Thursday is called *Gruendonnerstag* (Green Thursday). Many people think that the word *gruen* stands for the color, but this is not so. It derives from the ancient German word *greinen*, meaning "to cry or moan." Nevertheless, *Gruendonnerstag* will have its green lunch.

The evening of Holy Thursday finds us in our Sunday best around the dining-room table. Standing, we listen to the Gospel describing the happenings in the Upper Room. On the table is a bowl with "bitter herbs" (parsley, chives, and celery greens), another bowl with a sauce the Orthodox Jews use when celebrating their Pasch, and plates with unleavened bread (matzos can be obtained from any Jewish delicatessen store, but can also be made at home).

Unleavened Bread

1½ cups flour	1 egg, slightly beaten
¼ tsp. salt	½ cup butter
⅓ cup warm water	

Mix salt, flour, and egg. Add the water, mix dough quickly with a knife, then knead on board, stretching it up and down to make it elastic until it leaves the board clean. Toss on a small, well-floured board. Cover with a hot bowl and keep warm ½ hour or longer. Then cut into squares of desired size and bake in 350-degree oven until done.

Then comes the feast-day meal of a yearling lamb roasted, eaten with these bitter herbs and the traditional sauce. Each time we dip the herbs in the sauce, we remember Our Lord answering sadly the question of the Apostles as to who was the traitor: "He that dippeth his hand with me in the dish, he shall betray me." Afterwards the table is cleared and in front of Father Wasner's place is put a tray filled with wine glasses and a silver plate with unleavened bread. While breaking up portions of bread, he blesses the bread and wine individually and hands it to each one around the table and we drink and eat, remembering Our Lord, Who must have celebrated such a "love feast" many times with His Apostles. This was the custom in His days; just as we in our time will give a party on the occasion of the departure of a member of the family or a good friend, the people in the time of Christ used to clear the table after a good meal and bring some special wine and bread, and in the "breaking of the bread" they would signify their love for the departing one. The first Christians took over this custom, and after having celebrated the Eucharist together, they would assemble in a home for an *agape*, the Greek word for "love feast." To share bread and wine together in this fashion, therefore, was not in itself startling to the Apostles, but the occasion was memorable on this first Holy Thursday because it was Our Lord's own great farewell.

As we thus celebrate the breaking of the bread around our table at home, we keep thinking of the words He had said immediately before: "A new commandment I give unto you: That you love one another, as I have loved you. . . ."

Every Holy Thursday night spent like this knits a family closer together, "careful to keep the unity of the Spirit in the bond of peace, one body and one Spirit . . . one Lord, one faith . . ." as St. Paul wrote to the Ephesians.

On Good Friday Holy Mother Church gives her children a beautiful opportunity for a profession of faith: the adoration of the cross. Behind the priests and altar boys follows the whole congregation. We remove our shoes when we go to adore the cross. Three times we prostrate ourselves as we come closer, until we finally bend over and kiss the feet of the crucified. As we, the church choir, follow right behind the priest, we sing during the rest of the adoration. Our songs are the heartrendingly moving *Crux fidelis* by King John of Portugal, and Eberlin's *Tenebrae factae sunt*, of such haunting beauty.

When the adoration of the cross is finished, the candles on the altar are lighted, the cross is most reverently taken up from the floor and placed on the altar, and a procession forms to get the Blessed Sacrament from the "Altar of Repose." During this procession the hymn *Vexilla Regis* is sung. And then follows a ceremony that is not a real Mass, although it is called the "Mass of the Pre-Sanctified." The priest consumes the Host that was consecrated the day before. On the anniversary of Our Lord's death—the bloody sacrifice—the Church does not celebrate the symbol of the unbloody sacrifice. After the official service is finished, the altar is stripped again. The tabernacle is left open, no vigil light burns in the sanctuary. But in front of the empty tabernacle lies the crucifix on the steps of the altar, and the people come all during the day for adoration.

In Austria another custom was added. At the end of the official service the priest would carry the Blessed Sacrament in a monstrance, covered with a transparent veil, and expose it on the side altar, where a replica of the Holy Sepulchre had been set up with more or less historical accuracy, with more or less taste, but always with the best of will. Like the crèche around Christmas time, so the Holy Sepulchre on Good Friday would be an object of pride for every parish, one parish trying to outdo the other. The people in Salzburg used to go around at Christmas time and in Holy Week to visit the Christ Child's crib and the Holy Sepulchre in all thirty-five churches of the town, comparing and criticizing. There would be literally hundreds of vigil lights surrounding the Body of Christ in the tomb of rock, which was almost hidden beneath masses of flowers. There would be a guard of honor, not only of the soldiers, but also of firemen in uniform and of war veterans with picturesque plumed hats. I still remember the atmosphere of holy awe stealing over my little heart when as a child I would make the rounds of churches. There in the Holy Sepulchre He would rest now, watched over by His faithful until Holy Saturday afternoon.

Here in America we have found another lovely custom: people going from church to church not on Good Friday but on Holy Thursday. On that day, the churches are decorated with a profusion of flowers, as a sign of love and gratitude for the Holy Eucharist. The contrast with the bare churches the day after, on Good Friday, is all the more striking and gives a tremendous feeling of desolation.

Good Friday is a very quiet day with us. There is little to do in the kitchen, since fasting is observed rigorously on this day. We have no breakfast, and all that is served for lunch, on a bare table without tablecloth, is one pot of thick soup, *Einbrennsuppe*, which everyone eats standing up in silence. There is little noise around the house. Talking is restricted to the bare essentials, as it would be if a dearly beloved were lying dead in the house. As we are so privileged as to have a chapel in our house, we use the day when the holy house of God is empty and desolate to clean and polish all the sacred vessels and chalices and the ciborium, the monstrance, candlesticks, and censer.

The vigil light before the picture of the Blessed Mother in the living room is also extinguished, because on Good Friday Christ, the Light of the World, is dead.

From twelve until three, the hours of Our Lord's agony on the cross, all activity stops. We sit together in the empty chapel before the cross and spend these hours in prayer, meditation, and spiritual reading. From time to time we rise and sing one or the other of the beautiful Lenten hymns and motets.

On Holy Saturday, a new stir of activity starts in the kitchen. Eggs are boiled in different pots containing various dyes—blue, green, purple, yellow, and red. Every member of the household who wants to participate in this art takes some eggs to his or her room, after they have dried, to work on them in secret. One takes some muriatic acid with which she etches the most intriguing patterns out of the colored foundation. It is quite popular in our house to etch the first line of Easter songs—staves, notes, and words.

Our cleverest artist sits with paint and brush, and under her fingers appear pictures of an Easter lamb, or of Our Risen Saviour Himself, or of the Blessed Mother, or of the different patron saints of the family. Sometimes they turn out to be little gems.

Others fasten dried ferns or little maple leaves or other herbs around the eggs before they are boiled in dye. When these leaves are finally taken off, the shape of the flowers and herbs remains white, while the rest of the egg is colored. This is easily done and looks very pretty.

These eggs first appear on trays and in bowls on Easter Sunday morning at the foot of the altar for the solemn blessing of the food. Afterwards, they will be distributed at the solemn Easter breakfast.

Paschaltide

EASTER NIGHT

W E CANNOT be grateful enough that the Holy Father, Pius XII, has given back to us the ancient Easter Night! Even as children we felt that something was not quite as it should be when the Church broke out early in the morning of Holy Saturday in the threefold Alleluia, while the Gospel told us that Our Lord was resting in the grave to rise on Easter Sunday morning. Now the word of the Holy Father has put things straight and Holy Saturday has regained its ancient character. Apart from the one choir rehearsal for Easter, it is quiet around our house, everybody busying himself with preparations for Easter inside and outside. Some are getting flowers and candles ready to be put into the chapel upon our return from the parish church after midnight. Others are working out a new scheme of decorating the dining room for the greatest family meal of the year—the Easter breakfast. Practically everybody is preparing some special Easter eggs for someone else. In the late afternoon it is time for Confession, and after supper we sit together with the booklets containing the rites of Easter Night, reading and discussing the beautiful texts of this most holy liturgy. An air of expectancy is descending over the house and family which can only compare to Christmas Eve.

With the exception of one person who has to stay behind to guard the house, everybody piles into the cars to be down in Stowe a little before eleven. Invariably a voice out of the group will remind us: "Don't let's forget the lantern and the bottle for the Easter water."

Many of the traditions and customs, as I have related them so far, are centuries old, handed down from father to son. In the celebration of the Easter Night, however, we are experiencing the making of a tradition, and that is something precious, too.

As we come down to the little parish church in Stowe, we see people arriving from all sides. We are all silently waiting outside around a little pile of wood logs in front of the church door. Now comes the altar boy and, with a lighter—it is prescribed that the new flame should be made with flint—he sets fire to the wood. Meanwhile the whole community is congregated, a few hundred people waiting in the crisp air of the early spring, under the starry sky, for the "Feast of Light" to begin. Now a solemn little procession approaches from the dark church—the altar boy, our pastor, and our Father Wasner as deacon carrying the Paschal candle. First the new fire is blessed by the pastor. Then he turns solemnly to the Paschal candle around which this "Feast of Light" centers. With a knife the priest cuts a cross on the candle. Then the first and last letters of the Greek alphabet, the Alpha and Omega, and finally the numbers of the year, in this form, while he says:

Christ yesterday and today
the Beginning and the End
Alpha and Omega
His are the times
and ages
To Him be glory and dominion
Through all ages of eternity
          Amen.

Then he fixes five blessed grains of incense in the cross on the Paschal candle, saying:

By His holy
and glorious wounds
may He guard
and preserve us
Christ the Lord.
                Amen.

The deacon lights a small candle from the new fire and presents it to
the pastor, who solemnly lights the Paschal candle, saying:

May the light of Christ
In glory rising again,
Dispel the darkness of
Heart and mind.

All of us are holding unlighted candles, and now the procession forms
and enters the church. First comes the altar boy with the cross, then
the deacon with the lighted Paschal candle, then the pastor, the rest of
the altar boys, and finally the people. At the threshold of the church,
the procession stops. The deacon raises the candle and sings *Lumen
Christi* (Light of Christ) while all of us, genuflecting toward the
candle which represents Christ, the Risen Saviour, answer *Deo
gratias* (Thanks be to God). After the first *Deo gratias* the pastor
lights his candle from the Paschal candle. In the middle of the church
we are stopped again by the deacon, who repeats, one tone higher,
Lumen Christi. After the second *Deo gratias* the rest of the clergy
present and the altar boys light their candles. When the deacon
reaches the sanctuary, he chants for the third time, again a tone
higher, *Lumen Christi*, and at this *Deo gratias* the rest of the people
light their candles from the new holy light. The deacon places the
candle on a stand and in the warm glow of the many flames he sings
in a jubilant tone the most beautiful hymn of praise, the ancient
Exsultet.

    With this, the *Lucernarium* (the Feast of Light), the first of the
three major parts of the Easter Night, is completed and all the candles
of clergy and people are extinguished. Now begins the second part,
the baptismal service. Once more the priests change their white

vestments for violet and read at the altar four lessons. After each lesson the deacon admonishes the people, *Flectamus genua*, whereupon the congregation kneels down in silent prayer until he bids them, *Levate*.

After the four lessons, priests and people start to sing the Litany of All Saints. The Litany is sung as far as "*Omnes Sancti et Sanctae Dei, intercedite pro nobis.*" Then it is interrupted. In the middle of the sanctuary, next to the Paschal candle, a large vessel with water is prepared, which the priest now blesses most solemnly—the Easter water. Every family wants to take a bottle of this most holy water home. Therefore, a large quantity is set aside for the use of the faithful. Into the rest the holy oils are mingled, turning it into baptismal water. If anyone is waiting to be baptized in this holiest of nights, this is the moment when the baptism would be conferred right there in the sanctuary.

Then the vessel with the baptismal water is carried by the deacon, followed by the rest of the clergy in procession, over to the baptismal font. While the procession returns in silence to the sanctuary, the candles of clergy and people are lit again, the priests change from purple back to white, and the pastor steps over to the Paschal candle, facing the people, and prepares them for the most important moment of the year: ". . . Therefore, my dearest Brethren, now that the Lenten observance is over, let us renew the vows of our Holy Baptism, by which we have of old renounced Satan and his works, and also the world, which is the enemy of God, and promised to serve God faithfully in the holy Catholic Church." And then he asks us gravely:

"Do you renounce Satan?"

And the whole church resounds with the answer: "We do renounce him."

"And all his works?"

"We do renounce them."

"Do you believe in God, the Father Almighty. . . ."

"And in Jesus Christ. . . ."

"And in the Holy Ghost. . . ."

After the third thunderous "We do believe," we may rightly be convinced that our baptismal innocence is restored. When the meaning of all this dawns on one for the first time, one feels shaken to one's innermost being.

"Let us now with one voice pray God as Our Lord Jesus Christ has taught us to pray," says the pastor, and a renewed congregation, "born again by water and the Holy Ghost," says the Lord's Prayer.

All this happened to us once when we were infants and our godparents gave the answers in our name and held the baptismal candle for us. Now we are privileged once a year to renew these vows while holding the candle ourselves. This is truly a holy night!

Kneeling down, we finish the litany together with the priest, and then comes the third part—the Eucharist service, the midnight Mass.

Every year we repeat that the greatest reward for being a singing family comes when we can sing these jubilant Alleluias at the Easter Mass!

After the official liturgy is fulfilled, there still comes for us the observance of some ancient religious customs that belong to the liturgy of the home. In the lantern we take home some of the new blessed Easter light, with which we shall relight the vigil lamp at home. The bottle we fill with Easter water, and on the way out of church we take some of the blackened logs from the Easter fire and preserve them at the fireplace, where they work as sacramentals in times of danger from storms and lightning.

We try to keep up the customs we learned from the people in the Alps when they say the sorrowful mysteries of the rosary on Good Friday. Toward three o'clock of that day the father of the house goes to the corner where the vigil light burns before the crucifix and gravely blows it out; then he pours water on the fire in the fireplace. No flame is allowed around the house between the hour of Our Lord's death and His Resurrection, in honor of Him Whom we call the Light of the World.

When we return, therefore, in the Easter Night with the blessed light in the lantern, the vigil light is lit from it and also the fire in the fireplace, and all the holy-water fonts are filled with Easter water.

ALLELUIA
Philip Hayes, 1738-1797.

FOUR PARTS. ALLEGRO MODERATO

REJOICE, O REJOICE, HEAVENLY QUEEN

Sixth (Hypolydian) mode. This Antiphon replaces the "Hail Mary, Queen in Heaven" from Easter to Trinity Sunday.

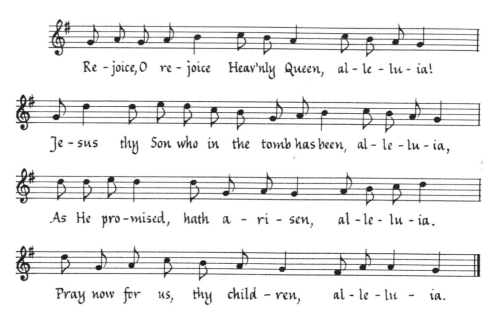

Re - joice, O re - joice Heav'nly Queen, al - le - lu - ia!

Je - sus thy Son who in the tomb has been, al - le - lu - ia,

As He pro - mised, hath a - ri - sen, al - le - lu - ia.

Pray now for us, thy child – ren, al - le - lu - ia.

THREE WOMEN AT BREAK OF DAY

Text and melody, Munich Hymnal, 1586.

Three wo - men at break of day had

joined With spi - ces so sweet Him to a –

noint, Christ Je - sus, whom they laid in the
tomb. He had a - ri - sen in ear - ly
morn. Ky - rie e - lei - son.

2. The Vir--gin Mary pure and mild,
   Had shed many tears throughout the night,
   For Jesus the Christ, her Son and Lord.
   He is our Saviour, He God's own Word.
   Kyrie eleison.

3. Christ Jesus, our Lord and Master dear,
   In glory aris'n Thou doest appear.
   Ah, give to me through Thy passion's power
   Eternal glory in my last hour.
   Kyrie eleison.

EASTER HYMN

Text and melody, Hymn Book, Cologne, 1623.

ALLEGRO

Christ is a - ri - sen glo - rious, God is a - gain vic -

to - rious. Let all be joy - ful sing - ing, with

al - le - lu - ia ring - ing, in cym - ba - lis, in

cym - ba - lis be - ne - so - nan - ti - bus, in

cym - ba - lis   be - ne - so - nan - ti - bus.

2. Hell has itself confounded,
   Satan is fast impounded.
   Let all be joyful singing,
   With alleluia ringing,
   In cymbalis, in cymbalis benesonantibus,
   In cymbalis benesonantibus.

3. Death cannot sting nor scar us,
   Sin shall no longer mar us.
   Let all be joyful singing,
   With alleluia ringing,
   Alleluia, alleluia, allealleluia,
   Alleluia, allealleluia.

4. God will to peace restore us,
   Shed Grace and Glory o'er us.
   Let all be joyful singing,
   With alleluia ringing,
   Alleluia, alleluia, allealleluia,
   Alleluia, allealleluia.

EASTER EGGS!

Text and melody from the traditional Easter Song, "Dalalin, Dalalin, po Yaichenki," in Rimsky-Korsakov's *Russian National Songs*, 1875. Translation, *Oxford Book of Carols*, by permission of Oxford University Press.

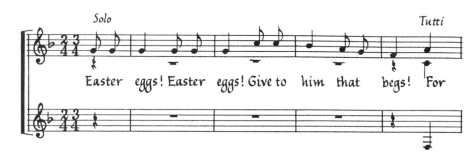

2. To the poor, open door,
   Something give from your store!—Refrain

3. Those who hoard, can't afford,
   Moth and rust their reward!—Refrain

4. Those who love freely give,
   Long and well may they live!—Refrain

5. Eastertide, like a bride,
   Comes, and won't be denied.—Refrain

EASTER DAY

Following a custom going back to the tenth century, all the kinds of food that were forbidden during the weeks of Lent are arranged in baskets and the Church has a special blessing to be pronounced on this food on Easter morning by the priest—the meat and eggs and butter, salt and Easter bread. We remember how in small country churches these baskets would be placed on the Communion rail, and how in larger communities the people would hold them in their arms while the priest, after pronouncing the blessing, would go down the aisle sprinkling holy water over the food.

This is what singles out the Easter breakfast from among all other meals of the year—that we partake of this solemnly blessed food. Ham and Easter bread and colored eggs and many, many flowers and pussy willows and silken ribbons give the table a festive look. Artistically painted eggs are usually kept by the owners throughout the year, but the simply colored eggs are now used for "*Eierpecken.*" Around the table everyone takes an egg in hand, and now, by two's, they try to "peck" the other one's egg first. The one who indents the other's egg, while his own remains uncracked, harvests the cracked egg. The one who finally has the most is hailed as victor.

In the old country all the big feasts, but especially Easter, are accompanied by "*Boellerschiessen.*" The young men use old fashioned heavy rifles, and particularly in mountainous parts of the country where the echo takes up those cannon-like detonations, they add tremendously to the festive character of the day.

And there's still another thing—the Easter fire. On all the heights and summits innumerable bonfires are lit in honor of the Risen Lord.

For Easter Monday there is an old custom, still very much alive in the old country, which might well be duplicated here, even though Easter Monday is not generally a holiday, as it is in Europe. In honor of the Gospel of the day, which tells of the two disciples who went to Emmaus and met Our Lord on the way, Easter Monday became a visiting day. Wherever there are old or sick people, they are visited by young and old.

The Sunday after Easter we still remember as White Sunday, for it was the day when the little children were led in a small procession by the rest of the parish into the church for their First Communion.

In the weeks between Easter and the Ascension there are four days set aside where the Church has her children go out into the fields and pastures chanting the litany of All Saints and asking God's blessing for a good harvest and as protection against hailstorms, floods, and droughts. One day is the feast of St. Mark, April 25th, and the other three days are called "Rogation Days" and are the Monday, Tuesday, and Wednesday preceding the Ascension, which always falls on a Thursday. We always make these outdoor processions up on our mountain. The very first hue of green is appearing in the meadows, the birds are singing in the woods again, and the whole atmosphere is one of spring and hope.

PENTECOST

On Ascension Day begin the nine days of waiting and preparing, together with the Apostles and Mary, the coming of the Holy Ghost. These are the days when families should discuss the "Gifts of the Holy Ghost" and the "Fruits of the Holy Ghost" evening after evening. As I look back over the years I marvel at how different these discussions were every year, always full of surprises, partly because there were different people participating—guests of the family or new friends of the children—who do not ordinarily hear the workings of the "Gifts of the Holy Ghost" discussed around the family table.

We devote one whole evening to each one of the gifts. First is the Gift of Knowledge, offered to help us in our dealings with inanimate and animate created nature, with things and people. It teaches us to make use of them wisely, and to refrain from what is dangerous for us. As we consider a typical day, we discover that this gift is needed from the very moment of awakening, when we have to part from the created thing "bed." The younger ones discover that the Gift of Knowledge helps them to remember that they have to make use of such created things as the toothbrush and the shower. In fact, there is hardly a moment of the day in which we do not have to make decisions about using something or dealing with somebody, and when we do not need the immediate help from the Holy Spirit to carry us safely through the day.

The second evening is devoted to the Gift of Understanding, which is extended to us for the understanding, with mind and heart, of revealed truth as we find it in Holy Scripture and the liturgy, and in the breviary. This gift we need for our hours of prayer and meditation. It fulfills the Lord's promise: "The Holy Spirit whom the Father will send in my name, He will teach you all things" (John 14:26).

The third evening is devoted to the Gift of Counsel, which helps us to distinguish, in every moment of our life, what is the will of God. This gift we also need when someone turns to us for advice. It is most necessary to parents and teachers, priests, and all persons in authority. But above all it should help us to make the right choices in everyday life—even in such minor matters as "Should I do my homework now or later? Should I see this movie or not?"

The Gift of Fortitude helps us to overcome our own will. This may start with such seemingly small matters as jumping out of bed the moment we had intended to do so; with giving up smoking or candies and cookies for certain times; with keeping silence when we might have a sharp answer ready; with doing little things for others at the cost of our own comfort; and it may lead to the ultimate test—aiding us in joining the thousands of contemporary martyrs who are called to lay down their life for God. Again, a gift that is needed throughout the day!

The Gift of Piety does not sound particularly attractive, until we realize that it infuses our hearts with a special kind of love, directed toward everything belonging and related to God: all persons consecrated to His service—the Holy Father in Rome, bishops and priests, missionaries, nuns, and lay brothers—and all things set aside for God only, such as church and altar, chalice and monstrance, vestments, and the sacramentals in our home—rosaries, holy water, medals. This precious gift also makes us eager to devote time to the service of God. It helps overcome morning laziness when it is time for Mass. It makes us want to visit our hidden God once in a while in church. In other words, it instills the interest for the supernatural in our souls. How could we do without it!

When we come to the Gift of the Fear of the Lord, there is always someone to raise the argument: "This I don't understand. That is the spirit of the Old Testament, of the chosen people who were trembling before Jehovah so that they said to Moses, 'You go up the mountain and talk with Him—we are afraid.' But the New Testament teaches us to say 'Our Father,' and Our Lord says, 'I don't call you servants any more, I call you friends!' One isn't afraid of one's father or one's friend! What do I need the Gift of Fear for?" It is then that something very tender and beautiful comes to light. If a person loves another one very much, you may often hear him say: "I'm afraid to wake him up, he needs his sleep"; or, "I'm afraid to disturb him." In other words, love is afraid to hurt the beloved one. The Gift of Fear should lead us to a state of mind which makes us afraid to sin because it would hurt Him.

The Gift of Wisdom, finally, seems to sum up all the Gifts of the Holy Spirit, just as charity sums up all His fruits. If we ask throughout all our days for the other Gifts of the Holy Ghost and cooperate with them, if we examine our conscience every night about the use we made of them—wisdom will grow in our hearts. This wisdom has nothing to do with ordinary human intelligence, with knowledge learned in schools and from books. One doesn't even have to be able to read and write in order to become wise. Once in a while one meets an old lay brother or lay sister, an old farmer in the country, or some bedridden person, who may not be learned in the eyes of the world, but may impress us deeply by a true wisdom expressed in all simplicity.

At the end of the seventh day we have all renewed our conviction that we cannot lead a truly Christian life without the special aid of the Holy Ghost, that we have to ask for it as we start each day, and be faithful to it as we go through the day. Children, with the generosity of young hearts, are remarkably responsive to this suggestion.

The eighth day of the novena is dedicated to the "Fruits of the Holy Ghost" as they are enumerated in St. Paul—especially the first three: love, peace, and joy. On this day we always call to mind the admonition of one of our dearest friends, Reverend Father Abbot, to take the word of Our Lord literally, that "by their fruits thou shalt know them." In every individual soul, in every family or community we should watch whether the fruits are the fruits of the Holy Ghost, whether love, peace, and joy prevail.

On the last day of the novena we meditate together on the two great hymns, *Veni, Sancte Spiritus* and *Veni, Creator Spiritus.* Through our previous discussions, these texts are seen in a new light, and the repeated *"Veni, veni"* ("Come, Holy Ghost, come") really rises from longing hearts. And when, during High Mass on Pentecost Sunday, priest and community kneel down at the solemn text of the Gradual, *Veni, Sancte Spiritus,* we feel the miracle of the first Pentecost repeated in our hearts, filled by the Holy Ghost in response to the intensity of our *Veni.*

In the old country, ancient Pentecost customs are still alive. On the Saturday before Pentecost Sunday the young men go out with long whips, cracking them with special skill to produce a noise called *Pfingstschnalzen*. This is followed by *Pfingstschiessen*, done with the same ancient guns that are used for shooting on Easter and other festivities. In some valleys people walk barefoot up into the mountains through the dew, calling for the Holy Ghost. In the Alps, cattle decorated with wreaths and garlands are sent up to the high pastures, accompanied for a little way by most of the villagers.

Many of the old churches throughout the Alps have a hole in the ceiling above the altar through which, on Pentecost Sunday, during High Mass the "Holy Ghost dove" is let down into the church. On Ascension Day, the statue of the Risen Lord is lifted on wires after the Gospel to disappear in the same opening, which brings the mystery of the day very close to all children, big and small. In some parishes the Risen Lord, at the end of the Mass, sends gifts down from heaven—apples and cookies and candies for the children, and flowers and green branches for the grownups, and everybody tries to take at least a leaf or a petal home.

This brings us to the end of the holy Paschal season. The octave day of Pentecost, known as Trinity Sunday, is dedicated to the Blessed Trinity. While in the first centuries the Easter Communion had to be received on Easter Sunday, the Church later extended "Easter Time," which now begins on Ash Wednesday and ends on Trinity Sunday.

Once a family has celebrated the year of the Church faithfully from the First Sunday in Advent, feasting and fasting together, until the fullness of the Holy Ghost crowns their efforts throughout the days of Pentecost, it will be a very happy family indeed.

TO THEE, THE HOLY GHOST, WE NOW PRAY

The text of this invocation of the Holy Spirit is by Berthold
of Regensburg (d. 1272). The melody, inspired by the Gregorian "Veni Creator," goes back to the 13th century. Published
in the oldest Catholic Hymn Book, of Michael Vehe, in 1537.
Sing this hymn three times, each time a tone higher.

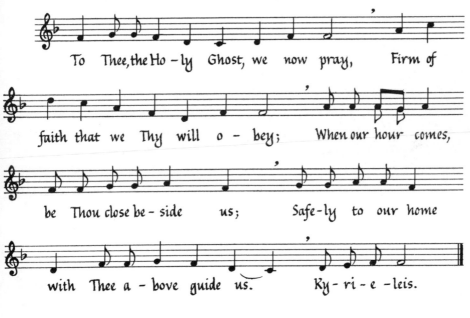

To Thee, the Ho - ly Ghost, we now pray, Firm of
faith that we Thy will o - bey; When our hour comes,
be Thou close be - side us; Safe-ly to our home
with Thee a - bove guide us. Ky - ri - e - leis.

The Green Meadow

WITH every passing year I realize more deeply how joyful our religion is. The more one penetrates into what it means to be Catholic, the fuller life becomes.

There is one great art that we are taught from our childhood and for which we cannot be grateful enough, and that is how to celebrate feasts. The little ones grow up hearing again and again: "Today is the feast of St. Joseph." "Next week is the feast of the Annunciation . . . the feast of St. John . . . the feast of the Holy Family . . . the feast of the Assumption." And these are not words only. Soon the children discover that these days have a truly festive character. Later, when they grow up and learn to use their own missals, they find that Holy Mother Church prepares a feast for us almost every day of the year. Naturally, these feast days are not equally important. Two of them, the anniversaries of Our Lord's Resurrection and of the Descent of the Holy Ghost, are of such magnitude and solemnity that the Church assigns a whole week to them. She wants to teach her children to take *time* for celebrating. What a necessary lesson for us of the fast-living twentieth century, when time has become money and the most important event in people's lives—their wedding —has been reduced from the ten-day celebration of old to a ten-minute formality at the Justice of the Peace!

For Easter and Pentecost the Church permits no other feast to interfere. This is called "a privileged octave of the first order." There are other great feast days, such as Epiphany and Corpus Christi,

Christmas, the Ascension, the feast of the Sacred Heart, and the feasts of the Blessed Mother, which also have an octave, and at least a commemoration of the feast is made each day.

If the first place is given to the feasts of Our Lord, the second is given to those of the Blessed Virgin Mary. Then come the holy angels, and they are followed by the saints who had a share in the plan of the Incarnation, as St. Joseph, St. John the Baptist, Peter and Paul and the other Apostles, whose feasts are always celebrated with special solemnity.

Then we are told to celebrate as a feast the dedication of churches, the anniversaries of the martyrdom of the saints, the commemoration of holy popes, bishops, teachers of the Church, confessors, virgins and all holy women. According to their importance these feasts will be more or less solemnly celebrated; but even a simple feast day is a *feast day.*

Once in a while there is a day in the calendar when we do not celebrate a feast. This is called a "ferial day." During most seasons these are few and far between, and it is all the more striking, therefore, to come to the six weeks of Lent and find that the Church has prepared a special mass for every ferial day and wishes her children to refrain from celebrating feasts during these weeks of penance. That makes the great Alleluia, which introduces the feast of the Resurrection, all the more jubilant.

Living through this cycle of festive events every year, one cannot help but learn that one should not just live one's life, or spend one's life, or go through one's life, but *celebrate* one's life. Whether the days are filled with bliss or mourning, we have learned to live almost each one as a special feast day. As the Introit of many a Mass bids us: "*Gaudeamus omnes in Domino, diem festum celebrantes.*" ("Let us all rejoice in the Lord, celebrating this festival day.")

If the time from the First Sunday in Advent until Pentecost seems like one long uninterrupted celebration of the greatest mysteries of our faith, the time from Pentecost to the end of the Church Year appears much more sober.

This second half of the Church Year is referred to in Austria as

"The Green Meadow," because of the green color of the vestments on the Sundays after Pentecost, whereas, until then, they had been violet, red, or white. If the festive character of the first part of the year is comparable to the mountain chains of the Alps or Andes, the single feasts in the months after Pentecost are like isolated peaks towering above the green meadow.

CORPUS CHRISTI

On the Thursday after the octave of Pentecost falls the feast of Corpus Christi—the feast of the Holy Eucharist. The actual anniversary of the institution of the Blessed Sacrament is celebrated on Holy Thursday, but on this day the Church cannot summon the proper festive mood, because of all the other happenings following the Last Supper, which she also has to commemorate. For this reason she has instituted a special feast day for this event. In the old country this used to be *the* great feast day at summer's beginning, with its distinctive feature the solemn procession, after the High Mass, in which the Blessed Sacrament was carried through the streets and over the fields and meadows. Such a Corpus Christi Day belongs among our most beautiful memories.

The day before, the big boys of the village cut young trees in the woods, usually birch, and plant them on either side of the road along which the priest will carry the Blessed Sacrament. From the village inn you hear the brass band having a last rehearsal, while mothers pin-curl the hair of their little girls. Everybody is preparing his finery for the great day. The Association of Voluntary Firemen come in their best uniforms and brass helmets. The war veterans will also be in uniform with big plumed hats. The big girls are making garlands by the yards which will span the street. All windows will be decorated, houses and families vying with each other: the best carpets, flanked by candles and flowers, are hung out the windows and statues and holy paintings are exhibited on them. Early in the morning freshly cut grass is strewn thickly on the road. Four times the procession will come to a halt, the priest will sing solemnly the beginning of one of the four Gospels and each time there will be Solemn Benediction. At those four spots altars are erected and decorated with trees and greenery and a profusion of flowers and candles. A great deal of love and care and time goes into these preparations.

Then comes the great day. The church choir gives its best at the Solemn High Mass and all the people attend from the mayor to the smallest child, for everybody wants to accompany Our Lord on His triumphal way. The procession is headed by an altar boy carrying a crucifix, followed by all the school children—the girls in white, their veils held in place by wreaths of flowers, looking for all the world like so many little brides; the boys wearing a wreath of flowers on their left upper arm over their Sunday-best, just like "best men." Then come the different confraternities with their banners and costumes. In the towns the convents would send every member they could spare. There would be the blue Vincentian Sisters with their coronets, looking like a group of doves, the white Dominican nuns, the brown Carmelites of the Third Order, the black Benedictines followed by the brown Franciscans, then the Mission Fathers and the bearded Capuchins followed by the secular clergy in their liturgical vestments. They are all like the heralds of the great King Who is following now under the richly embroidered baldachin carried by the four most important men of the community. The pastor carries the monstrance with the Blessed Sacrament. Two little girls are throwing flower petals out of baskets directly at the feet of Our Lord. Little altar boys alternate in ringing silver bells and swinging the censer from which rise billowing clouds, enveloping the Sanctissimum. On the right and on the left are marching soldiers carrying guns as if on parade. Behind the Blessed Sacrament follows the church choir, then a detachment of firemen, the war veterans in uniforms, and the rest of the community. At the very end of the procession comes the brass band playing hymns while everybody joins in the singing. The highlights for everybody, young and old, are the moments of benediction with the priest raising the monstrance for all to see and the soldiers lifting their guns and shooting their salute, while from the outskirts cannons resound with a thundering echo. I cannot remember a single occasion when it rained on Corpus Christi Day. From a cloudless blue sky a hot June sun would shine. At the end of such a triumphal procession everyone from the oldest grandfather in a plumed hat to the smallest flower girl would be in a truly festive mood.

In the new world, we naturally found a different Corpus Christi celebration. In Philadelphia, where we stayed for the first two years, we took part once in a Corpus Christi procession which went around the church grounds. In the second year we acted as church choir at the convent where our little girls went to school, walking around their big garden. It was all very solemn and moving and devout. But as soon as we were up on our hill in Vermont, we obtained the bishop's permission for an outdoor procession. Now we put up two altars, Hedwig cuts the grass early in the morning with a scythe, and all of us accompany Our Lord on His way over the fields and pastures and back home through our cemetery.

THE FEAST OF THE SACRED HEART

Eight days after Corpus Christi follows the feast of the Sacred Heart. After Jesus had died for us on the Cross, He wanted to do even more—to give His last drop of blood. And so the Roman soldier pierced His heart with a lance. One would think this would have convinced all later generations of their Redeemer's love. But the "Prince of this world" saw to it that Christians in the course of time became forgetful of this love. To remind us, Jesus in 1675 appeared to a humble little nun in France, St. Margaret Mary, all aglow and radiant, the Risen Christ of Easter Sunday. On His breast she saw His heart all afire. Our Lord pointed to it, saying, "Behold, this heart which has loved men so much," and He told her to spread the news: everyone who would venerate this symbol of the Divine Heart He would reward with divine generosity.

> I will give them all the graces necessary in their state of life.
>
> I will establish peace in their houses.
>
> I will comfort them in all their afflictions.
>
> I will be their secure refuge during life, and above all in death.
>
> I will bestow a large blessing upon all their undertakings.
>
> Sinners shall find in My Heart the source and the infinite ocean of mercy.
>
> Tepid souls shall grow fervent.
>
> Fervent souls shall quickly mount to high perfection.
>
> I will bless every place where a picture of My Heart shall be set up and honored.
>
> I will give to priests the gift of touching the most hardened hearts.
>
> Those who shall promote this devotion shall have their names written in My Heart, never to be blotted out.
>
> I promise them in the excessive mercy of My Heart that My all-powerful love will grant to all those who communicate on the first Friday in nine consecutive months the grace of final penitence; they shall not die in My disgrace nor without receiving the Sacraments; My Divine Heart shall be their safe refuge in this last moment.

As our home is called "Cor Unum" and our motto for daily life that we want to be one heart and one soul, we chose the feast of the Sacred Heart as our family feast. On that day, after a Solemn High Mass and the feast-day breakfast, we have our yearly family conference. We report on all the doings of the past year, we talk about the plans of the coming year. This is the day for every one of us to say whether he or she wants to stay in the family choir known as the Trapp Family Singers for another season; whoever wants to get married or whoever wants to do something on his own—this is the day to say so. This custom comes from the old country. Many families have their family day on the feast of the Holy Family in January, some on the feast of St. Joseph, who was a family man.

THE FEAST OF CHRIST THE KING

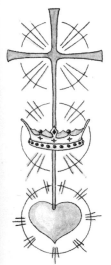

There is one more feast of Our Lord which comes late in the year, on the last Sunday of October—the feast of Christ the King. According to the Church calendar, this seems like a recent feast instituted only in 1925. But one glance at the Gospel of the day shows us that it actually goes back to the first Good Friday when Pilate said to Jesus, "Art Thou the King of the Jews?" and Jesus answered, "Thou sayest it." This carries us many hundreds of years back into the Old Testament, when God's chosen people were living in a theocracy, ruled by judges, God speaking to them through the mouths of His prophets. Then one day the Jewish people wanted "to be as the others"; they saw all the neighboring peoples ruled by kings, and so they went to their prophet Samuel and asked him: "Give us a king to judge us as all other nations have." Reluctantly Samuel told the Lord what the people demanded of him, and God pled with his unruly people. "Tell them," He said, "what will befall them if I give them a king. He will take their sons and make them his soldiers. He will take their men to work his fields. He will take their daughters to be his cooks and bakers. He will take their best fields and vineyards and olive orchards. Moreover, he will take a tenth from all they grow and also from their flocks." But all His pleading availed Him little. The people stubbornly repeated, "Nay: but there shall be a king over us. We want to be like other nations and our king shall judge us and go out before us and fight our battles for us!" Finally the Lord said to Samuel, "Hearken to their voice and make them a king." And then it happened as God had foretold it. The kings throughout the ages took their men and women, their young men and maidens, their best fields and meadows and a tenth of all they grew and of all their flocks, and many a time the people cried to the Lord to take away a bad king, but the Lord would not hearken any more.

As if now in our time God had opened His ear once more to the pleading of His people, He presents His Son to us as Christ the King, Whose Kingdom is not of this world, Who is above and beyond all human politics, but Who is eager to be our King so that we may be His people. The forerunner of our modern feast of Christ the King is the age-old feast of the Epiphany, when the three Magi fall down prostrate and adore the King, bringing among their gifts gold to give Him.

On the feast of Christ the King, our table decoration might relate to the character of the day. Together with the little ones, the mother could make a golden crown either of cardboard or of gold foil, as centerpiece of the table.

THE FEASTS OF MARY

Two months in the year are especially dedicated to the Blessed Mother—the month of May and the month of October. Special devotions to Mary during May go back to medieval times. October is the month dedicated to the rosary, since the feast of the Most Holy Rosary is celebrated on October 7th. In these months the Blessed Mother's statue or her picture in the living room are daily decorated with fresh flowers and candles. The family adds one or the other prayer, mornings and nights, such as the *Salve Regina* or the *Memorare* or the *Magnificat*. It is traditional throughout the Catholic world to sing hymns in honor of Mary the Mother of God. Some of those we have included here. We love especially the round by Mozart. It is composed only on the two words with which the Angel greeted Our Lady the first time and which countless millions of lips have repeated since: "Ave Maria." "Meerstern" (*Stella Matutina*) has been received enthusiastically by everyone who has heard it sung even once.

AVE MARIA

W. A. Mozart. Canon in four parts.

AVE MARIA DEAR

Text and melody, *Echo Hymnodiae Coelestis*, 1675.

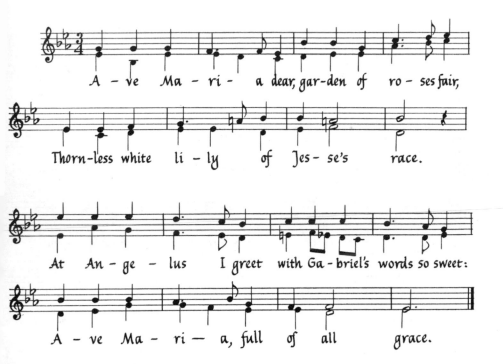

A - ve Ma - ri - a dear, gar-den of ro - ses fair,

Thorn-less white li - ly of Jes - se's race.

At An - ge - lus I greet with Ga - briel's words so sweet:

A - ve Ma - ri — a, full of all grace.

2. Thou hast the Father's Son, Maria, Purest one,
   In thy chaste womb given protection,
   Jesus the Holy Child, Who sinners all defiled
   Himself has saved from their destruction.

3. Therefore, O Mother mild, pray for us to thy Child,
   Ask that our sins may be forgiven:
   After this life of tears, Maria, through thy prayers,
   Gain us eternal joys of heaven.

SALVE REGINA

Text by Hermann the Cripple, 1013-1054, monk of Reichenau;
melody fifth (Lydian) mode.

Hail, Queen most no - ble, Hail Thou Mo - ther most mer - ci - ful, Thou life's true sweet - ness, Thou our hope, we greet Thee. To Thee we're cry - ing, from pa - ra - dise ban - ished children. To Thee we come weeping, sor - row - ing and sigh - ing in this dark and tear - ful val - ley. Ah, turn Thine eyes, Ad - vo - cate, in mer - cy, turn in lo - ving and kind com - pas - sion These Thine eyes up - on us sin - ners. And Je - sus, the blessed fruit of Thy

vir - gi - nal womb, show un - to us when our e - xile
is en - ded. Thou'rt cle - ment, Thou'rt
lo - ving, Thou — art sweet, O Vir - gin Ma - ry.

'TIS SAID OF OUR DEAR LADY

"An old invocation when one is on a pilgrimage to **Our
Blessed Lady**"—Text and melody from the hymn book of
Nikolaus Büttner, 1602.

'Tis said of Our dear La - dy, a ho - ly dream had
she: Be - neath her heart un - spot - ted there
grew a love - ly tree. Ky - ri - e e - lei - son.

2. *And as the tree its shadow extended far and near,
E'en so Our Lord Christ Jesus became our Saviour dear. Kyrie eleison.*

3. *Then Our most Blessed Lady a tiny Child did bear,
So let us now with singing our happiness declare. Kyrie eleison.*

STELLA MATUTINA

Pilgrim hymn from Paderborn, Germany. As no translation
has proved satisfactory, we are giving the Latin version.

Stel - la ma - tu - ti - na, A - ve Ma - ri -
De - i Nos om - nes ad - ju - va!
a! Laus ti - bi et vi - ta,
Nos - tra Do - mi - na! Ma - ri - a, Ma - ter

2. *Rosa sine spina, Ave Maria!*
   A Deo electa,
   Nostra Domina!—Refrain

3. *Perduc nos ad Christum, Ave Maria!*
   Filium dilectum!
   Nostra Domina!—Refrain

BEAUTIFUL, GLORIOUS

Text, 18th century; melody, *Geistliche Gesänge*, Einsiedeln, 1773.

Beau-ti-ful, glo-ri-ous, o'er all vic-to-ri-ous,
Thy child for-e — ver, lea-ving Thee ne — ver

Love-ly, thrice bles — sed hea-ven-ly Queen.
Bo-dy and spirit I e — ver have been.

My life de-spi — sing, Thee on-ly pri — zing,

All that I am, that I e-ver can be

give I, my Mo — ther Ma-ri-a, to Thee.

2. *Thou art all full of grace, in Thee sin has no place,*
   Thou, O Maria, Thou only art fair.
   And to Thy majesty nothing can wanting be,
   All that is perfect and lovely is there.
   Vase of election, of all perfection,
   Thou art, O Virgin, so wondrously made,
   That God Thee chose and in glory arrayed.

A SINGLE BRANCH THREE ROSES BORE

From Silesia, 1840.

A single branch three ro-ses bore, O Ma-ri - a. They bloom upon the heav'nly shore, O Ma-ri - a. O Ma-ri-a, see we raise A thou-sand times our hymns of praise, Our hymns of praise.

2. *What in her womb does Mary bear? O Maria.*
   As roses bloom an infant fair. O Maria.—Refrain

3. *What on her brow does Mary bear? O Maria.*
   A crown that God bestowed on her. O Maria.—Refrain

VIRGIN BLESSED, THOU STAR THE FAIREST

ANDANTE   Italian Laude, 15th century.

Vir-gin bles-sed, Thou star the fair-est, Brigh-ter none in hea-ven shi-ning, Ne-ver could my tongue be tel-ling, O Ma-ri-a Thy beauty 'ra-rest.

2. *Virgin blessed, enthroned for ever,*   *To my erring ways bring comfort,*
   Daughter of the Lord and Mother,   *Let Thy mercy forget me never.*

agnificat anima mea DOMINUM

Once I came across a family custom among friends of ours which I found so lovely that I want to mention it here. They treated their May altar in a most original way. As their apartment was too small to allow for an extra table, they put the statue of the Blessed Mother on their grand piano. The decorating was a family affair. Everybody could contribute what his heart urged him to bring. Throughout the month of May the smaller children would bring flowers which they had picked on their way home from school. Sometimes they placed their favorite toy at the feet of the Blessed Mother for a particular evening. It was the most irregular, but also the most lovingly arranged May altar I have ever seen.

From the old country we took with us the longing to pray at a wayside shrine in honor of Mary. As there were no shrines here, we simply made one ourselves. During the month of May we often walk in a little procession over to this shrine, saying the rosary and singing hymns. There is no reason why people could not make a shrine of their own in their gardens—under an apple tree, behind a rose bush—and during the month of May the whole family could once or twice a week have their May devotion outside.

We must lose the inhibition that our friends or neighbors "might mind" such exhibition of our faith. In all the years we have been living in America, time and again we have found that the average American is a most tolerant person when he senses that what you do is the outgrowth of an inner conviction. Take this instance: Three times a day the bell in our chapel rings the Angelus, whereupon everybody in the house stops talking, drops any work he is doing at that moment, and says the age-old prayer, "The Angel of the Lord declared unto Mary." At the words, "And the Word was made flesh," we make a genuflection. After the Angelus we make the sign of the cross and return to whatever we have been doing before. Most of the time people of various religious affiliations are among our guests, but not one single time have I seen the flicker of a smile or any sign of criticism or contempt or whatever else we timid Catholics might be expecting. We are put to shame by every Mohammedan. At certain times of the day he takes his little prayer rug and kneels down, facing the east, to say his prayers, not minding what anybody might think or say. What his prayer toward the east is for the Mohammedan, the Angelus might be for us Catholics. If the circumstances of our life allow it, why not start this custom next month of May and keep it up ever after?

The day of the Assumption, August 15th, is the oldest and most important of all the feast days of the Blessed Mother. In the old country it is also known as "Great Flower Day." All the women and girls come to church on this day with their arms full of neat bundles of herbs, which they put down in the sanctuary at the Offertory procession. On this feast day the Church blesses the herbs immediately preceding Mass. The priest, standing before the altar and facing the people, pronounces a long and solemn blessing at the end of which the herbs are sprinkled with holy water and are incensed. There are special herbs which traditionally have to be included. Days before the feast the people are collecting them in the meadows and woods. Every family sends one such bundle to be blessed. Afterwards it will be kept in the corner at home near the picture or statue of the Blessed Mother. In cases of sickness a leaf is dropped into the food of the patient and during heavy thunderstorms one of the herbs is put into the fire on the kitchen stove—it is a sacramental and is meant to protect us in body and soul.

The connection between the feast of the Assumption and the blessing of herbs is told in an old legend: When Mary the Mother of Jesus felt that her end was drawing near, she sent her guardian angel to summon the Apostles, who had gone out into the world to preach the Gospel of her Son, Our Lord Jesus Christ. When they received the summons, they came in a great hurry and were just in time to witness the happy death of their dear Mother. Everyone had come except Thomas. He was three days late. When he heard that the

Blessed Mother had been resting in the tomb for days, he cried bitterly and pled with the Apostles to open the tomb once more and let him glance at the beloved features. The other Apostles yielded to his plea, but as they opened the tomb, they found it filled with flowers, which gave out a heavenly scent. On the place where they had laid the body there was only the shroud left—the body had been borne up to heaven by the angels, where it was joined by the holy soul of the Mother of God. According to the legend, all the flowers and herbs on earth had lost their scent after Adam and Eve committed the first sin in the Garden of Eden. On the day of the Assumption of the Blessed Mother, however, the flowers were given back their scent and the herbs their power to heal.

If the day of the Assumption is the oldest and most important feast of the Blessed Mother, the Church also remembers lovingly all the major events of her life. These days used to be days of obligation in the early Church. Only the feast of the Immaculate Conception on December 8th is such today in the United States. But every Catholic home in which the Mother of God is venerated will celebrate reverently these days: her birthday on September 8th and her feast day on September 12th (the feast of the Holy Name of Mary). These could be celebrated in almost the same way as the birthday and feast day of the mother of the house: her place (statue or picture on the wall) decorated with flowers or evergreens, according to the season; vigil lights; a special song added in her honor at the family's morning and evening prayers; a little celebration with perhaps some reading (a story, a poem, a psalm from her office, a hymn out of the breviary, etc.) in the evening. There are many ways to honor someone we love.

When Mary was three years old—so we are told by tradition—her parents presented her in the temple, where she remained for the next few years, together with other young children from the first families (she was a princess of the royal house of David). These girls, while serving God, learned to spin, weave, and embroider the vestments and curtains around the temple. Helping to take care of the many priests on duty, they also learned to prepare food. They had to read long passages from Holy Scriptures, like the Book of Psalms; and they had to learn by heart parts of the Prophets and Proverbs. Thus, long before the angel talked to Mary, she knew of the tragic life and the cruel death predicted for the Messiah. Every year on the twenty-first of November, when we celebrate the feast of the Presentation, the Church draws our thoughts to that part of Mary's life.

The anniversary of the day when the angel said, "Hail, Mary, full of grace"—words repeated millions and millions of times ever since—the twenty-fifth of March, the Annunciation, is perhaps the most widely known feast of the Blessed Mother. From the earliest days of Christianity, in the catacombs of Rome, up to today, painters throughout the ages have tried to capture this greatest moment in human history, while composers have kept the "Ave Maria" ringing ever new.

When St. Luke tells us that, after the angel left, Mary "went with haste over the meadows" to visit her aged cousin, Elizabeth, the Church wants us to remember this in the feast of the Visitation on the second of July, so that we may always feel assured that Mary is ever ready to come to our aid.

According to Jewish teaching, Mary's child, being the firstborn son, belonged in a special way to God. Forty days after his birth, every male child had to be redeemed by the offering of a lamb, if the parents were well to do, or a pair of doves if they were of simpler means. At the same time the mother had to bring a purification offering while she was presenting her boy, through the priest's hands, to God. This twofold holiday in Mary's life we celebrate with her on the second of February. Because old Simeon would exclaim that this Child was "the light to enlighten them that sit in darkness," the Church blesses in a most solemn way the candles for the use of the altar. Therefore the day is popularly known as Candlemas Day. On this day every family takes the candles and vigil lights they will use during the year into the church for the solemn blessing. On the evening of this feast of the holy light, many of the blessed candles are lit for family prayer, thus leading the children into the world of holy symbols.

The next time the Church shows us the Mother of God, and also our Mother, is as "Mater Dolorosa"—the Mother of sorrows. The painters have pictured her as such usually either standing under the cross or with the dead body of her Son resting in her arms. When we celebrate the "Mater Dolorosa" on the fifteenth of September in our families, we might tell our children that her suffering did not start on Good Friday but at the very moment when she said to the angel, "Behold the handmaid of the Lord, be it done to me according to thy word." As at the moment of her solemn *fiat* the Son of God started His earthly existence under her heart, all the words from the prophets and Psalms took on a new meaning for her. She knew that this little Child, Who would be born nine months hence, would be the "Man of Sorrows" of Holy Scripture. Any mother who holds a baby in her lap, or watches the first steps and the growing up of the older ones, should meditate on what it would mean to her if she knew that her little child would one day be cruelly tortured by a seething mob. For this is what Mary knew while she fondled the newborn baby. When she kissed the little hands and feet, she felt her lips already stained by the precious blood gushing forth from deep wounds; when she tended carefully the hair of the little boy, she knew it would be matted one day by cruel thorns and blood and sweat and the spittle of His enemies. Such thoughts and meditations will bring our Mother much closer to our families.

When the children see the mother decorate the altar of the Blessed Mother in the home on the seventh of October, they will ask, "What feast is today, Mother?" Then we mothers will tell our children, as soon as they are old enough to understand, the story of the apparition of the Blessed Mother to one of her sons, St. Dominic; this story shows how we can please her most: while saying ten "Ave Marias," we should meditate in our heart on the happenings of her earthly life. There are the joyful ones—the Annunciation, the Visitation, the Nativity of our Lord, His Presentation in the Temple, and His Finding again in the Temple; there are those which tear her heart asunder in most bitter suffering: her Son's agony in the Garden, His scourging at the Pillar, His crowning with thorns, His carrying the heavy cross, and His bitter end on Calvary; and there are her moments of triumph when He rose from the dead, ascended to Heaven, sent the Holy Ghost, took her up to Heaven, and, finally, crowned her as Queen of Heaven. Thus the Blessed Mother—so legend tells us—taught St. Dominic how to say the rosary. On that day we wish to say it solemnly together—maybe all three, the joyful mysteries in the morning, the sorrowful after lunch, and the glorious at night. It is amazing how even very little children get the feeling for mental prayer if they are shown pictures of the appropriate mysteries while the grownups say the rosary.

On the sixteenth of July there is another chance for the children to ask Why, and that is when they see the mother decorate Mary's picture. There is another touching story we can tell our children to make them understand how solicitous our heavenly Mother is for our eternal salvation. Once she appeared to another of her sons, St. Simon Stock, Father General of the Carmelite Order in England. She showed him the scapular, the straight piece of cloth falling down from the shoulders to the feet in back and front, with an opening for the head. This was a part of the clothing of men and women in the time and country of Our Lord. Mary said to St. Simon, "Whoever will wear this garment, and die clothed in it, I shall come myself and take him up into heaven on the Saturday after his death." This is known as the "Sabbathine Promise" and on the sixth of July we celebrate the feast of Our Lady of Mt. Carmel (popularly known in Europe as the Scapular Feast). Simon Stock added the scapular to the habit of the Carmelite monks and nuns. For practical use among lay people it was cut down until it reached its present-day size—just two little pieces of brown cloth worn over the shoulders on white tape. One by one, as the children grow up, they will be enrolled in the scapular. What a consolation to parents and children if they know that their beloved ones, whom God called to Himself, died clothed in the scapular!

PILGRIMAGES

In Austria, the main part of our family celebration of the feasts of the Blessed Mother would be a pilgrimage to "Maria Plain." If the weather permitted, we would walk from our home down to the river and along it, an hour and a half, to the foot of the mountain on which the three-hundred-year-old pilgrimage church stood at the edge of an old grove. All the way we would say the rosary, one rosary after the other. At the foot of the mountain we would light candles which we had brought along. With burning candles, we would say one more rosary, singing the pilgrimage hymn after each decade. Then we would attend Holy Mass, receive Communion, place our candles on the big stand where many, many others were burning already. After Mass and Communion we would kneel for some time in front of the picture of the Blessed Mother for a heart-to-heart talk. And then one felt wonderful—light-hearted, strengthened, happy. Outside again we would invariably pause and take in the marvellous view across the ancient city with the high mountains in the background. But then one of the children would remind us that we had prayed now for a solid three hours on an empty stomach! For just such people was the *Kirchenwirt*, the Church Inn, very conveniently located a few hundred feet below on the slope. On the way to the inn we passed stands where they sell postal cards, candles, and more or less trashy little souvenirs. We all bought a few postal cards which we would write while waiting for our breakfast.

When we found ourselves in America, this was one of the things we missed most—that there were no famous old pilgrimage churches dotting the landscape, no wayside shrines to which one could make a pilgrimage as we were used to doing.

To make pilgrimages to hallowed places is a custom as old as mankind. We find it in India, China, with the old Babylonians, Greeks, and Romans. It comes from an urge that is deeply rooted in the human heart: to worship God in holy places designated by Him. For the Christian Rome and Jerusalem are the holiest places, and for two thousands years they have been what Mecca is to the Mohammedan: at least once in his lifetime he wants to go to the holy place!

Of course, these thoughts did not come to us as long as we were in Austria. There we just took pilgrimages for granted, like so many other things. But in America, when we started to wail and complain about the absence of hallowed shrines and our new American friends said, "What is all this talk about pilgrimages?" we found ourselves forced to do some thinking on the subject. It was then that we discovered that a pilgrimage is not predominantly a Catholic custom. Archeology has shown that certain places seem to have been hallowed throughout the ages—different peoples thousands of years apart choosing the same spot for their worship, whether they were Etruscans, Romans, or Christians.

Everybody knows about Lourdes and Fatima, but in addition to these world-famous shrines of the Blessed Mother, there are thousands of other places scattered all over the Christian countries where exactly the same thing happened: a soul in great distress prayed fervently to the Mother of God and, in a miraculous way, the plea was answered. In such places of miracle, churches were erected later. This is the usual origin of the pilgrimage centers as we know them all over Austria. From our home outside Salzburg there were as many as seven different ones which we could reach by bicycle or, in very grave necessity, on foot. In the old country, a hike of several hours is essential to a true pilgrimage. It is a very moving thing to have taken part in a pilgrimage of a whole village. The people would collect at one place (a custom that always reminds me of the *statio* of the daily Lenten Masses and of the time when the people of Rome used to meet in one place and walk in a solemn procession to the church where the day's Mass was to be celebrated). There the procession would form, led by an altar boy with a crucifix and guided usually by one of the parish priests. The people would alternately say a decade of the rosary and sing a hymn along the way until they reached a certain point in the vicinity of the shrine— usually at the foot of the hill or at a wayside cross if there was no hill. There they would all light their candles. The last part of the pilgrimage would be a crescendo of prayer and song. The inside walls of the pilgrimage churches are usually crowded with votive pictures and crutches, wax models of hands, arms, legs—indicating the cures that have been obtained in this holy place—and it is written in stone and wood and scribbled in ink and pencil all over the walls: Mary has helped, Mary will help again. This creates such an atmosphere of trust and confidence that merely to be there is soothing to

N.S. D GUADALUPE

the soul. As many people have said, returning from a pilgrimage, "Even if I hadn't received what I have asked for, the Blessed Mother has filled my heart with gratitude and happiness. Now I suffer gladly." This is one of the main secrets of Lourdes.

Another origin of a place of pilgrimage is very often the vow somebody took in a moment of great danger: If the Blessed Mother helps me through this, I am going to build her a chapel or a church. When the boys in our family went abroad as soldiers in the American Army, one of them took such a vow during the heat of battle: If he came home safely, he would erect a chapel to Mary, the Queen of Peace, on the highest point of our property. He did return safely, and for several years now he has been working on his chapel. It is a labor of love. Soon we hope to celebrate the blessing of the little sanctuary and then we can continue making our pilgrimages, either privately or in groups, lighting our candles at the foot of the hill, saying the rosary and singing hymns and obtaining graces through Mary who is called "Mediatrix of all Graces."

As our concert tours took us all over this vast continent we learned that the new world also has its holy places. "Good St. Anne" attracts the multitudes to Ste. Anne de Beaupré, St. Joseph to Montreal, the North American Martyrs have their shrine in Auresville, N.Y., the

Indian martyr, Kateri Tekakwitha, has hers in Caughnawaga, outside Montreal. The bodies of St. Rose and Blessed Martin de Porres attract pilgrims to Lima, Peru. But most of all the Blessed Mother hallowed a spot of her own choice by making Guadalupe the Lourdes of the new world.

THE ANGELS

Long before our little children learn to know Peter Rabbit, Donald Duck, Mickey Mouse, and Winnie the Pooh, they must be made familiar with their most faithful companion—their best friend, their guardian angel. The beauty of telling stories to little ones lies in their ready acceptance. They believe that their guardian angel is around all the time, day and night, and they will talk to him, greeting him in the morning, discussing things with him during the day, thanking him in the evening. When children grow up with a strong sense of a spiritual power at their service, instituted by God for the very special and sole purpose of being their very own helper and protector, such children need never be afraid, need never suffer from the modern ailment of insecurity. It is up to us mothers to bring about this early and very personal friendship with their guardian angel. The feast of the Holy Guardian Angel on October 2nd should be a big event in our nurseries.

Once children are familiar with the world of the angels they will eagerly listen to other "angel stories" such as the one about the great hero Michael (whose feast day is September 29th) and his battle with his brother-angel Lucifer, who refused to serve God and had to be thrown out of heaven into the abyss where there is "weeping and wailing and gnashing of teeth." A beautiful story is the one about the Archangel Raphael (feast day, October 24th), who was the friend and companion of young Tobias. Johannes Brahms set a lovely song about St. Raphael to music; we always sing it on that day.

And as we tell the children about the good angels, we shall also have to mention the bad ones who turned into devils. If the highest of them, Satan himself, dared to tempt Our Lord, who are we to think that it "can't happen to us" or that such stories belong to the Middle Ages and do not apply to modern times? What St. Peter says to all of us we must tell to the little ones as well: "Watch and pray, for the devil goes about like a roaring lion seeking whom he may devour."

SAINT RAPHAEL

Johannes Brahms, *Deutsche Volkslieder,* No. 7.

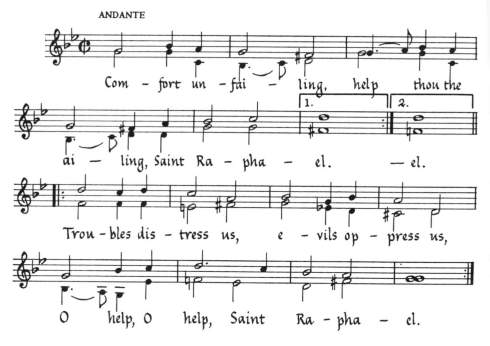

2. *While we are sleeping, watch thou art keeping, Saint Raphael.*
   Troubles distress us, do not forget us, O help, O help, Saint
   Raphael.

3. *For none damnation, for all salvation, Saint Raphael.*
   Sinners, repent ye, humbly relent ye, O help, O help, Saint
   Raphael.

THE SAINTS

I don't know what I would have done without the saints in bringing up our large family. Long before our children could memorize the Apostle's Creed and pronounce, "I believe in the Communion of Saints," they were already participating in it. Very early they had learned that the Communion of Saints is one large, happy family whose members have one thing in common: they want to go to heaven. Some of them, like ourselves, are still living here on earth, working hard to reach the goal. Very many, however, have already reached it. These are our big sisters and brothers, the saints. And there is still another group. As Our Lord has said once that nothing unclean can enter the Kingdom of Heaven, most of the souls, after they leave the body in death, are not found ready and have to be purified in Purgatory from the last stain of sin. Even while suffering, these souls are happy because they know that, for them, time with its great dangers is over and soon they will be forever united with their Lord and God.

"Be ye perfect even as your Heavenly Father is perfect," says Our Lord, and "This is the will of God—your sanctification," explains St. Paul. We mothers cannot begin early enough to make it seem quite natural to our little ones that we all—they and we—must strive to become saints just like. . . . And this is where our big sisters and brothers enter in. The most precious thing about the saints is that they were not born that way. They had their faults just as all of us do, and they had to work hard to overcome them. Some of them were quick-tempered like St. Peter or St. Francis de Sales; some even lied and stole and cheated their mother, as St. Augustine tells us about himself; some were quite wicked, like St. Paul or Mary Magdalene; others were meek and mild from the beginning, like little St. Thérèse and Dominico Savio. We parents could learn from the great eagerness with which the children take to certain TV programs or movies with Hopalong Cassidy or other popular performers that every young soul is a hero-worshipper. Children simply need someone to look up to, to imitate. Well, there is no

Hollywood hero who could not be easily outdone by one of the saints. Among that very large number of our big sisters and brothers who "made it" there is one for every kind of child. There are the Old Testament saints. Some of their stories are more exciting than all of Grimm's fairy tales. Think of the stories of Abraham when he goes up the mountain to sacrifice his only son; of King David and King Solomon; the prophet Jeremiah; Daniel in the lion's den; and Tobias with his friend, Raphael; not to forget our saintly first parents, Adam and Eve, whose feast the Church celebrates on the vigil of the birth of Our Lord, December 24th. There are the stories of the holy women—Judith, Ruth, and Esther; that exciting adventure story of Joseph in Egypt; and the harrowing tale of Job on the dunghill.

Then there are the New Testament saints—all the Apostles and the holy women. There are the many heroes from the time when Christianity was an underground movement: the martyrs of the first centuries, especially the young ones—the boy Tarcisius, who was killed as he was carrying the Blessed Sacrament secretly to the prisoners in Rome, the girls Agnes and Philomene and Cecilia. There are rich saints like King Louis of France and Queen Elizabeth of Hungary and Queen Margaret of Scotland. There are poor saints like Francis of Assisi and Benedict Joseph Labre. There are saints who were sick most of their lives, like Lydwina. There are saints who were famous for their jokes and laughter, like Philip Neri and Don Bosco. When we turn the pages of one of the books with a daily story about one of the saints, we find that there were holy boys and girls, holy mothers and fathers, holy lawyers, doctors, slaves, popes and priests, farmers and swineherds, tailors and bakers—just "holy everybody," as one of our children once said.

My husband had once taken great pains to tell a beautiful fairy tale to the children. When he had finished, the oldest asked, "Is all of that true, Father?" Slightly embarrassed, he had to admit that it was not, whereupon the child said, "Why did you tell us, then?" Often afterwards, when we came across tales of saints who had spent their lives sitting on a column, such as Simon the Stilite, or who flew through the air like Joseph of Cupertino, we would say that as a story this equalled any fairy tale but had the added advantage of standing the crucial test, "Father, was that true?"

First of all a child must be acquainted with his own patron saints, whose names were given to him at his baptism. Later on he will also learn about the patron saints in his immediate family, and in a large family like ours this will amount to a great number of stories. Then, by and by, as the child grows up and hears more about these big sisters and brothers, he will add some of his own liking. I told my children always to look for saints who had the same troubles and the same faults as they did and then to ask his or her intercession. He must know how it is. Whereupon one day one of the little ones said to me, "Mother, I know now why you choose St. Peter as your favorite saint. He could get so mad that he once even cut somebody's ear off!"

Throughout the centuries Christian people have adopted this same policy. They have searched in the lives of the saints and have chosen certain ones as patrons for certain ailments. There is, for instance, a group of fourteen saints particularly famous for their prompt intercession in special cases, known as the Fourteen Holy Helpers (Fourteen Auxiliary Saints). Here is the list, together with the attributes by which they are characterized in painting and sculpture.

(1) St. George (April 23rd), soldier-martyr. Always represented with the dragon he strikes down. He is invoked against the devil, and together with St. Sebastian and St. Maurice he is the patron of soldiers.

(2) St. Blaise (February 3rd), bishop, carries two candles crossed; he is invoked against diseases of the throat.

(3) St. Erasmus (June 2nd), martyr. His entrails are wound around a windlass. He is invoked against diseases of the stomach. Patron of seafarers.

(4) St. Pantaleon (July 27th), bishop. He is recognized by his nailed hands. Invoked against consumption. Together with St. Luke and Saints Cosmas and Damien, patron of doctors.

(5) St. Vitus (June 15th), martyr. He is recognized by his cross. Invoked against St. Vitus' dance and the bite of poisonous or mad animals.

(6) St. Christopher (July 25th), bears the Infant Jesus on his shoulder. Invoked in storms and against accidents in travel.

(7) St. Denis (October 9th), bishop, holds his head in his hands. Invoked for people who are possessed by a devil.

(8) St. Cyriacus (August 8th), martyr, wears deacon's vestments. Invoked against diseases of the eye.

(9) St. Acathius (May 8th), martyr, wears a crown of thorns. Invoked against headache.

(10) St. Eustace (September 20th), martyr, wears hunting clothes and is shown with a stag. Invoked against fire—temporal and eternal. Patron of hunters.

(11) St. Giles (September 1st), hermit, is recognized by his Benedictine habit and his hind. Invoked against panic, epilepsy, madness, and nightmares.

(12) St. Margaret (July 20th), martyr, keeps a dragon in chains. Invoked against pains in the loins. Patron for women in childbirth.

(13) St. Barbara (December 4th), martyr, is recognized by her tower and the ciborium. Invoked against sudden death. Patron of artillery men and miners.

(14) St. Catherine (November 25th), martyr, is shown with a broken wheel. Invoked by students, philosophers, orators, and barristers as "the wise counsellor."

In the old country, a picture of the Fourteen Holy Helpers is to be found in many a little wayside shrine or impressive pilgrimage church, such as Vierzehn-Heiligen in Bavaria.

It cannot be stressed enough that perhaps the most important books in the home, after Holy Scriptures, are those dealing with the lives of the saints. Besides the classic Butler, there are other collections. We always liked Omer Englebert's *The Lives of the Saints,** which gives the story of several saints for every day, thus providing one with many "true stories." Looking through those "Lives" becomes more and more fascinating as we realize the many links uniting these people of long ago with us in the twentieth century. To my amazement I discovered that there is a patron saint for practically every profession—though we have to distinguish between

* New York, David McKay Co.

saints appointed by the people themselves and others appointed by Rome. Thus the Holy Father, Pius XII, named St. Michael the patron of policemen, St. Albert the Great as patron for scientists, St. Alphonse Liguori as patron of Confessors, and St. Catherine of Siena as patron of nurses. He appointed Our Lady under her title of the Immaculate Conception as patroness of the soldiers of the United States, while his predecessor, Pius XI, made St. Thérèse of Lisieux patron of all missionaries, St. Aloysius patron of all young people, the famous Curé of Ars, St. Jean-Baptiste-Marie Vianney, the patron of parish priests. What I myself like best of all is that Rome appointed Our Lady of Loretto the patroness of aviators (obviously because she steered successfully the holy house of Nazareth through the air and had it land in Loretto, Italy, where it has been venerated since the Middle Ages).

Besides these "appointments" of patron saints, there are many chosen by the people. I never could find out why St. Anthony of Padua (June 13th) has to find lost objects for everybody around the globe or why St. Matthew (February 24th) is the patron of repentant drunkards. With other saints it is easy to see why some incident of their life or death was taken up by the people as indications that they should be invoked in special cases. Good St. Anne is the patron saint for mothers-in-law and domestic troubles; St. Florian (May 4th), who was a Roman soldier condemned to death as a Christian and drowned in the River Enns in Austria, is universally invoked to extinguish fires, obviously with the help of the water hallowed by his death; St. Bartholomew (August 24th), who was skinned alive, was made patron for all tanners and butchers. It is easy to see why the Holy Innocents (December 28th) are the patrons of choir boys and foundlings but rather hard to fathom why St. Margaret (July 20th) cures kidney diseases.

One of our children made a list once, "in case we need it," of saints to be invoked for special illnesses. Here it is:

Against fever—St. Hugh (April 29th)
Against epilepsy—St. John Chrysostom (January 27th)
Against burns and poisons—St. John the Evangelist (December 27th)

Against inflammations—St. Benedict (March 21st)

Against cough and whooping cough—St. Blaise (February 3rd)

Against consumption—St. Pantaleon (July 27th)

Against cold—St. Sebaldus (August 19th)

Patron of all the sick and dying—St. John of God (March 8th)

One of our boys got interested in patron saints for special professions. Here is his little list:

St. Jerome—patron of students (September 30th)

St. Isidore—patron of laborers (May 10th)

St. Ives—patron of lawyers, jurists, advocates, notaries, and orphans (May 19th)

The "Four Crowned Martyrs"—patrons of masons and sculptors (November 8th)

St. Francis de Sales—patron of writers (January 29th)

St. Gomer—patron of the unhappily married (October 11th)

St. Gregory the Great—patron of singers (March 12th)

St. Cecilia—patroness of musicians (November 22nd)

St. John the Baptist—patron of tailors (June 24th)

St. Paul—patron of rope-makers (June 30th)

If there are girls and boys in a family and one of the boys has made a list of various saints for different professions, the girls simply have to make a list of patron saints too. Ours found patron saints for animals:

Bees—St. Ambrose (December 7th)

Pigs—St. Anthony the hermit (January 17th)

Dogs—St. Rochus (August 16th)

Horses—St. Leonard (November 6th)

Asses—St. Anthony of Padua (June 13th)

Birds—St. Francis of Assisi (October 4th)

Fish—St. Anthony (June 13th)

And once in a while somebody would come running with a special discovery.

"Mother, look! We have enough girls in our family. I found a patron saint to obtain male children: St. Felicitas (July 10th)!"

"Mother, do you think Aunt Susan knows there is a saint of old maids—St. Catherine of Alexandria (November 25th)?"

They also found that St. Gaston is the patron of children who learned to walk very late, and they discovered a few very valuable saints for weather. If you want rain, pray to St. Odo; if you want sunshine, pray to St. Claire. But the head of the heavenly weather department is of course St. Peter.

And so it goes. If the children in a family become sufficiently interested in their big brothers and sisters, the saints, to start making such lists and finding out about the respective feast days, it is just as if one of their grown-up sisters were getting married and the new in-laws taken into the family. Their birthdays and feast days are noted down, the enlargement of the family circle is celebrated, and this, each time, is a happy occasion.

While close relations are kept up with a great many of the saints, some of them are singled out by the Church to be celebrated in a special way. There is, for instance, St. John the Baptist, whose feast is celebrated on the twenty-fourth of June. We learn that as far back as the eighth century bonfires were being lit in honor of the precursor of Christ—the *Johannesfeuer*—as a special solemnity. In the old world, the young people of the villages and towns take kindling wood up the mountains or outside of town to some beautiful spot on a river bank. Before it is lit a few words point out the significance of this fire at the height of the year, at the beginning of summer when the nights are shortest; and the symbolism of fire and light in relation to that radiant figure, the Baptist. "He was a burning and a shining light: and you were willing for a time to rejoice in his light" (John 5:35). When the flames are leaping up, everybody present joins in singing one of the old songs of the occasion. When the fire is burning low, everyone leaps over it—boys and girls holding hands and leaping by twos. Then they settle down around the fire for the fire-watch until the last spark has died out.

Soon afterwards, on June 29th, we celebrate the feast of St. Peter and St. Paul. The badge of St. Peter is the cock, in memory of the "thrice-crowing" of that animal. As St. Peter is the "Great Fisherman," his feast day is celebrated in many seacoast towns with great festivity. Boats are decorated with garlands and ribbons. There are races, and the chief dish is fish, of course.

In our extensive travelling throughout many countries over three continents we have come across many a saint who is very famous locally but of whom we otherwise might never have heard. One day in the year is set aside to remember them all—the ones whose names are mentioned in the calendar and the multitudes who stand around the throne of God. This is All Saints' Day, on November 1st. In the Epistle, St. John tells us about the vision he had of the "great multitude which no man could number, of all nations, and tribes, and peoples, and tongues, standing before the throne and in sight of the Lamb, clothed with white robes, and palms in their hands," singing praise to God.

The teaching of Our Lord in the Gospels tells us what makes a saint a saint: "Blessed are the meek . . . Blessed are they that mourn . . . Blessed are they that hunger and thirst after justice . . . Blessed are the merciful . . . Blessed are the clean of heart . . . Blessed are the peacemakers . . . Blessed are they that suffer persecution for justice' sake. . . ." Nothing is so encouraging as to consider, on All Saints' Day, those millions and millions around the throne of God who followed this teaching. Like St. Augustine before her, our Martina, when she was still quite little, said once on All Saints' Day, "As I think of it, Mother, if all those people could do it, why not we!"

ALL SOULS' DAY

Toward the end of the year, on November 2nd, the Church sets a day aside which is devoted to the suffering souls in Purgatory. Just as we turn to our big sisters and brothers, the saints, to intercede for us at the throne of God, the poor souls are also turning toward us: "Have pity on me, have pity on me, at least you, my friends, because the hand of the Lord has touched me" (Job 19:21; Office of the Dead). Helpless in themselves, since the purification they are undergoing is passive suffering, they can be helped by us. We can pray for them. We can offer up sacrifices and good works with the desire that God may accept them and, seeing in them the prayer and suffering rise from the Mystical Body of His only Son, hasten the delivery of those souls whom He deems worthy and ready for such help. On the day of "all the faithful departed" the Church reminds her children to listen to the message of the Scriptures in her liturgy and to do some thinking and meditating on Purgatory and the holy souls there.

We know Purgatory is a realm of twilight, so to speak—an in-between darkness and light, a place of regret and longing. Of the suffering which is undergone there, we are told that it is bitter and great, that it surpasses all imaginable suffering here on earth as an ocean surpasses a little puddle.

A knowledge of Purgatory we find already in the Old Testament. Two hundred years before Christ Judas Machabeus "making a gathering . . . sent twelve thousand drachms of silver to Jerusalem for sacrifice to be offered for the sins of the dead, thinking well and religiously concerning the resurrection, (for if he had not hoped that they that were slain should rise again, it would have seemed super-fluous and vain to pray for the dead) ; and because he considered that they who had fallen asleep with godliness, had great grace laid up for them. It is, therefore, a holy and wholesome thought to pray for the dead, that they may be loosed from their sins" (II Macc. 12:43-46).

All Souls' Day is a solemn day for families. We mothers must tell our children again about the Communion of Saints, which functions in the same way as life in a large family, where each member depends on the others. In this case, the poor souls depend on us. They depend on our love, but love does not consist in words only, it consists in deeds. The sooner the little ones learn to understand this, the better it is for their whole life. On All Souls' Day they will be encouraged to bring little sacrifices, to say special prayers. They will be told about the *thesaurus ecclesiae*, the golden treasure chest of Holy Church filled with the atoning sacrifice of Christ, the merits of the Blessed Virgin, of the saints—canonized and uncanonized—into which we may delve. It was given to Peter to bind and loosen, and his successor, making use of that very power, sets the conditions under which this can be done. One such disposition is the *toties quoties* indulgence: each time we visit a parish church on the second of November and say six "Our Fathers," six "Hail Marys," and six "Glorys," we may gain a plenary indulgence applicable to the poor souls.

All Souls' Day is also the date when we remind our children that on the solemn day of their baptism the Church lit the baptismal candle and said: "Receive this burning light and see thou guard the grace of thy baptism without blame. Keep the Commandments of God so that when the Lord shall come to call thee to the nuptials, thou mayst meet Him with all the Saints in the heavenly court, there to live forever and ever." This baptismal candle of our children we should wrap reverently and keep in a special place together with our own. If, as happened to us, these candles are no longer in the family (we could not take along such things from the old country), one can take candles blessed on Candlemas Day, tie the names of each child to a candle, and keep them in a special place. This is what we did. Only Johannes, being born in this country, has his own original baptismal candle. On All Souls' Day we take the candles out and look at them and remind each other to light our candle for any of us in case of sudden death, as a symbol that we want to die in our baptismal innocence, that the light which was kindled at that solemn moment has not been extinguished voluntarily by us. It is always a solemn moment when the children are called to think of their parents' death.

In the old country the great event of the day used to be the visit to the cemetery. First I have to describe an Austrian cemetery. Out in the country every village has its cemetery around the church; bigger towns have them on the outskirts. Every grave is a flower bed at the head of which is a crucifix, sometimes of wrought iron, sometimes carved in wood. Occasionally there are also tombstones. Families take care of their graves individually. People who have moved elsewhere will pay the cemetery keeper to do it for them. The German word for cemetery is *Gottesacker*, meaning "God's acre." In the summer it looks like a big flower garden. People are

constantly coming and going, working on their graves, or just praying for their loved ones. On anniversaries you will see vigil lights
burning and on All Souls' Day every grave will have its little vigil light
as a token that we do remember. People will flock out to the cemeteries in the early evening because it is such a sight—those many,
many flames and all the mounds covered with flowers. Slowly one
walks up and down the aisles, stopping at the graves of relatives
and friends to say a short prayer and sprinkle them with holy water.

When the father of our family died several years ago, we started
our own old-world cemetery. Soon one of his children followed
him and now there are two flower-covered mounds under the large
carved-wood crucifix. The lanterns are lit not only on the anniversaries and on All Souls' Day, but every Saturday night. A hedge of
rosa multiflora encircles this holy spot. Inside the hedge there is a
bench and we often sit there in the peace and quiet of our little acre
of God.

The Land Without a Sunday

OUR NEIGHBORS in Austria were a young couple, Baron and Baroness K. They were getting increasingly curious about Russia and what life there was really like. One day they decided to take a six-weeks trip all over Russia in their car. This was in the time when it was still possible to get a visa. Of course, at the border they were received by a special guide who watched their every step and did not leave them for a moment until he deposited them safely again at the border, but they still managed to get a good first-hand impression. Upon their return they wrote a book about their experiences, and when it was finished, they invited their neighbors and friends to their home in order to read some of their work to them. I shall always recall how slowly and solemnly Baron K. read us the title: "The Land Without a Sunday." Of all the things they had seen and observed, one experience had most deeply impressed them: that Russia had done away with Sunday. This had shocked them even more than what they saw of Siberian concentration camps or of the misery and hardship in cities and country. The absence of Sunday seemed to be the root of all the evil.

"Instead of a Sunday," Baron K. told us, "the Russians have a day off. This happens at certain intervals which vary in different parts of the country. First they had a five-day week, with the sixth day off, then they had a nine-day work period, with the tenth day off; then again it was an eight-day week. What a difference between a day off and a Sunday! The people work in shifts. While one group enjoys its lay off, the others continue to work in the factories or on the farms or in the stores, which are always open. As a result the over-all impression throughout the country was that of incessant work, work, work. The atmosphere was one of constant rush and drive; finally, we confessed to each other that what we were missing most was not a well-cooked meal, or a hot bath, but a quiet, peaceful Sunday with church bells ringing and people resting after prayer."

Here I must first tell what a typical Sunday in Austria was like in the old days up to the year before the second world war. As I have spent most of my life in rural areas, it is Sunday in the country that I shall describe.

First of all, it begins on Saturday afternoon. In some parts of the country the church bell rings at three o'clock, in others at five o'clock, and the people call it "ringing in the *Feierabend.*" Just as some of the big feasts begin the night before—on Christmas Eve, New Year's Eve, Easter Eve—so every Sunday throughout the year also starts on its eve. That gives Saturday night its hallowed character. When the church bell rings, the people cease working in the fields. They return with the horses and farm machinery, everything is stored away into the barns and sheds, and the barnyard is swept by the youngest farmhand. Then everyone takes "the" bath and the men shave. There is much activity in the kitchen as the mother prepares part of the Sunday dinner, perhaps a special dessert; the children get a good scrub; everyone gets ready his or her Sunday clothes, and it is usually the custom to put one's room in order—all drawers, cupboards and closets. Throughout the week the meals are usually short and hurried on a farm, but Saturday night everyone takes his time. Leisurely they come strolling to the table, standing around talking and gossiping. After the evening meal the rosary is said. In front of the statue or picture of the Blessed Mother burns a vigil light. After the rosary the father will take a big book containing all the Epistles and Gospels of the Sundays and feast days of the year, and he will read the pertinent ones now to his family. The village people usually go to Confession Saturday night, while the folks from the farms at a distance go on Sunday morning before Mass. Saturday night is a quiet night. There are no parties. People

stay at home, getting attuned to Sunday. They go to bed rathe
early.

On Sunday everyone puts on his finery. The Sunday dress i
exactly what its name implies—clothing reserved to be worn only o
Sunday. We may have one or the other "better dress" besides. W
may have evening gowns, party dresses—but this one is our Sunda
best, set aside for the day of the Lord. When we put it on, we in
variably feel some of the Sunday spirit come over us. In those day
everybody used to walk to church even though it might amount t
a one or two hours' hike down and up a mountain in rain or shine
Families usually went to the High Mass; only those who took car
of the little children and the cooking had to go to the early Mass.

I feel sorry for everyone who has never experienced such a long
peaceful walk home from Sunday Mass, in the same way as I feel sorry
for everyone who has never experienced the moments of twilight
right after sunset before one would light the kerosene lamps. I know
that automobiles and electric bulbs are more efficient, but still they
are not complete substitutes for those other, more leisurely ways
of living.

Throughout the country, all the smaller towns and villages have
their cemeteries around the church; on Sunday, when the High
Mass was over, the people would go and look for the graves of their
dear ones, say a prayer, sprinkle holy water—a friendly Sunday visit
with the family beyond the grave.

In most homes the Sunday dinner was at noon. The afternoon was
often spent in visiting from house to house, especially visiting the
sick. The young people would meet on the village green on Sunday
afternoons for hours of folk dancing; the children would play games;
the grownups would very often sit together and make music. Sunday
afternoon was a time for rejoicing, for being happy, each in his own
way.

Until that night at Baron K.'s house we had done pretty much the
same as everybody else. Saturday we had always kept as *Feierabend*
for Sunday. There was cleaning on Saturday morning throughout
the house, there was cleaning in all the children's quarters—desks

nd drawers and toys were put in order. There was the laying out
f the Sunday clothes. There was the Saturday rosary, and then—
arly to bed.

On Sunday we often walked to the village church for High Mass,
specially after we had started to sing. Later we used to go into the
nountains with the children, taking along even the quite little ones,
r we used to play an Austrian equivalent of baseball or volleyball,
r we sat together and sang some of the songs we had collected our-
elves on our hikes through the mountains. We also did a good deal
f folk dancing, we had company come or we went visiting ourselves
—just as everybody else used to do. And if anybody had asked
us why we began our Sunday on Saturday in the late afternoon,
why we celebrated our Sunday this way, we would have raised our
eyebrows slightly and said, "Well, because that's the way it's always
been done."

But when my husband and I were walking home that night from
Baron K.'s house, we realized that our complacency—so prevalent
among people in prewar days—had received a rude shock. It dawned
on us that we had taken something for granted that was, in reality,
a privilege: namely, that we lived in a country where Sunday was
not so much observed as it was *celebrated* as the day of the Lord.
This was a new way of looking at things, and the light was still
rather dim, but I can see now in retrospect that a new chapter in
our life as a Christian family began that very night.

We were lucky. The priest who stayed with us at that time, saying Mass in our chapel, and who had become a close friend of the
family, was in a very special way a "Sunday fan," as we teasingly
called it.

"I don't know what is the matter with Father Joseph," my husband had remarked to me at various times. "He always hints that
we don't make enough of the Lord's Day. Why, we stop work on
Saturday when the *Feierabend* begins; like everybody else, we get
ready for Sunday by preparing our Sunday clothes, going to Confession, reading the Epistle and Gospel. On Sunday we go to Mass
together with our children, we have a good Sunday breakfast, later
in the day we go visiting. If there's anyone sick among our friends,

we try to see him. We spend the day together as a family, as i
should be. We go for hikes with the children, or we play games, o
we have some folk dancing, or we make music. . . . I really don'
know what he means."

I do know now. It is true that we spent the Day of the Lord as a
family, praying, resting, and rejoicing together. I'm sure Father
Joseph did not object to that. But what he felt was that we did it
unthinkingly, as a matter of routine, because everybody in Austria
in those days did it like this. It had become a tradition. Father Joseph
must have sensed the great danger to a nation once people observe
religious customs only because "everybody does it" or "for hundreds
of years it has been done this way." He knew that every generation
has to rediscover for its own use the inheritance that has been
handed down from its ancestors. Otherwise all those beautiful old
customs, religious or other, lose their vitality and become museum
pieces. Father Joseph noticed that increasingly people were answering, when asked why they observed certain rites, "because we have
always done it that way," and he was alarmed. What he was most
concerned about, however, was the celebration of Sunday.

On the crucial night, we decided that we would get together
with Father Joseph the very next day and ask him to tell us all we
didn't know about Sunday. So we asked him to have a cup of coffee
with us. If he had a weakness, it was for coffee. With this, one could
lure him always. Smiling in anticipation, he took his cup when my
husband asked quite casually, "Father, would you mind telling us
all about Sunday and why you were so upset when we once wanted
to go to a movie on Saturday night, or when Rupert and Werner took
their bicycles apart on a Sunday afternoon?"

And now something unexpected happened. Father Joseph put his
cup down, went over to my husband, took his hand in both of his,
shook it heartily, and said with a voice audibly moved: "Thank
you, Georg, thank you for this question. I have been praying for this
moment for a long time!" And then he added, "I won't be able to
tell you *all* about Sunday, but we can at least start. . . ."

How well I remember it all—for I have re-lived this moment many
times since, only now it is I who take Father Joseph's place and listen

some more or less impatient good Christian questioning: "May ask what is the matter with you and your Sunday and what you re always fussing about?"

Father Joseph was right. He was not able to tell us everything in his first session. When my husband and I saw that we were on the threshold of a great discovery, we suggested that we let the older children participate. From then on we spent many, many evenings, and every Saturday evening, listening to Father Joseph explaining to us "all about Sunday."

He began by giving us a history of the development of the Sunday in Apostolic times. The first Christian community in Jerusalem remained faithful to the observation of the Sabbath Day as well as to the prayer in the Temple, as we know from the "Acts of the Apostles." But at a very early date the Apostles themselves must have instituted a new custom: after the close of the Sabbath, the Christians remained assembled in prayer and meditation and chanting of hymns to spend the night in vigil and to celebrate the Holy Eucharist in the early hours of the morning. As their Lord and Saviour had risen from the dead on the day after the Sabbath—"*in prima Sabbathi*," as the four Evangelists call that day—the first Christian community celebrated, not the seventh day, like the Jews, but the first day of the week, and so made every Sunday into a little Easter.

Then Father Joseph suggested we read in the "Acts of the Apostles" about those times when the young Church was increasingly faced with the perplexing question whether non-Jewish converts from paganism should be obliged to observe all the Jewish laws too, as, for instance, the observation of the Sabbath Day. And we read about the Council of Jerusalem around the year 50 A.D., when the Apostles decided that the Sabbath Day need not be observed any more. From then on the "Acts of the Apostles" reveal that those two sacred days begin to conflict. St. Paul still uses the Sabbath to teach in the synagogues about Jesus Christ, but he also organizes and presides over the Sunday celebration in the new Christian communities of the Greek world. The conflict becomes more open toward the end of the first century when the Christians cease to call their holy day "Sabbath" and name it "the Lord's Day," or "Dominica," instead. We find the first mention of "the Lord's Day" in the first chapter of the Apocalypse, where St. John says that his vision took place on "the Lord's Day." St. Ignatius of Antioch will use this term again in his letters to the young Christian communities. In the *Didache,* one of the earliest descriptions of the lives of the first Christians, we find the sentence, "But on the Lord's Day, when you have gathered together, break bread and give thanks."

In the days of St. Ignatius, who was martyred around the year 110, the Christians went one step further in their detachment from the Old Testament, which now was considered as a symbol and prefiguration, to be fulfilled in the New Testament. St. Ignatius writes that "it is monstrous to talk of Jesus Christ and to practice Judaism." In his day, the Sunday already had completely replaced the Sabbath of the Old Law as the weekly sacred day.

Then Father Joseph told us about the situation of the Christians outside the Holy Land. In the Roman Empire, every ninth day was a holiday. The Christians in Rome and Asia Minor were unacquainted with the main characteristic of the Jewish Sabbath Day— the complete cessation of work. Living under Roman law, it would have been impossible for them to stop working, especially in periods of persecution. We now came to see that, while the act of worship of the Sabbath of old consisted in abstaining from work, the act of worship of the Sunday of the Christians consisted, from the very beginning, in the celebration of the Eucharist. To assist at the sacrifice of the Mass was strictly indispensable. Even in times of persecution, when the Church had to go underground, the Holy Eucharist was celebrated secretly in private homes early in the morning. Every Sunday morning the Christians risked their lives in order to celebrate the Holy Eucharist. We know that Rome had its very efficient secret police and that during the first three hundred years of Christianity, thousands of martyrs sacrificed their lives. What a great day Sunday must have been to those people!

One of our children asked, "Father Joseph, didn't the early Christians always celebrate Holy Mass in the catacombs?" and he answered that the most recent archeological findings show that the most ancient churches in Rome were erected on the foundations of private homes; the common belief is now that the catacombs, as public cemeteries, would have been too easy a target for the Roman police. Only occasionally Holy Mass was said there, over the body of one of the martyrs; the usual Sunday celebration would take place secretly in private homes.

Next we saw the Church rising in the beginning of the fourth century. The times of persecution were over; a new life was beginning. The ceremonies of the Holy Eucharist did not have to be held in secret and in the dark of the night; they could now be celebrated in broad daylight. This led to important changes in the celebration of Sunday. From now on the Sunday liturgy begins to develop more and more. In the fourth century the great Roman basilicas were erected in different parts of the big city.

At this phase of our study, we spent many evening hours with Father Joseph, listening to his explanation of the origin of the station churches. On the main Sundays of the year, such as Pentecost and the Sundays following the Ember Days, the Pope used to go in solemn procession to celebrate Holy Mass in one of these basilicas, accompanied by all the clergy and faithful of Rome.

Father Joseph's enthusiasm was contagious. He knew Rome as well as we knew our house and garden. He brought a box with postal cards along, showing all the ancient basilicas, all the station churches, details from their architecture, and especially the mosaics. When our concert tour several years later took us to Rome, it was like coming home to a familiar place.

In the fourth century the Sunday took on a new character. Now the Church could afford to declare it the official holy day of the week. In the sixth century we see that the cessation of work has already become a law.

A new change became apparent with the flowering of monasticism. From the very beginning, the monks took up the idea of hourly prayer throughout the day and of special prayers at midnight. This had a decided influence on the celebration of the Sunday vigil, which had always been observed but was now becoming a general practice. After having spent the greater part of the night from Saturday to Sunday and the morning hours in prayer and meditation, the

Sunday necessarily took on the character of a day of rest. Now the Sunday had taken over completely the function of the Sabbath. It had become both a day of worship and a day of rest.

Parallel with the development of the Sunday went the development of the liturgical year. In the beginning, the Christians celebrated only one feast: that of Easter. It began on Good Friday, rose to its height on Easter Sunday and was continued during fifty days, the Paschal season, which ended with Pentecost Sunday. The first four hundred years of Christianity did not know the season of Lent, but the Christians fasted every Friday, and later every Wednesday also.

In the fourth century a new feast came to be celebrated: the anniversary of Christ's birth; and just as Pentecost was the completion of Easter, so the feast of the Epiphany became the conclusion of the festive Christmas time. The liturgy of the fourth century, then, was centered on two big feasts: Christmas and Easter. As time went on, both of these feasts developed further and added weeks of preparation, the season of Lent and the season of Advent. Now the liturgical year was formed. Its development had a most important influence on Sunday. So far the Sundays had repeated over and over again the celebration of the same mystery: Christ rising from the dead. Now, however, each Sunday took on a significance of its own. No longer were there just "Sundays," but Sundays during Advent, Sundays during Lent, Sundays after Easter, and Sundays after Pentecost. Some took on a special name, such as "Gaudete Sunday," "Laetare Sunday," "Good Shepherd Sunday," "Rogation Sunday."

Of course, our children wanted to know: "And how about the feasts of the saints?" And we learned that during the first few hundred years only a martyr was considered worthy of being commemorated on a special feast day. On the anniversary of his martyrdom Holy Mass would be said, but only at the place where his body rested. This restricted the feasts of the martyrs to specific places. Beginning with the fourth century, saints that had not died the death of martyrdom were given a special feast. Such a feast doubled the octave of the day; hence the name "double feast." For many centuries, however, the sanctoral cycle was considered secondary to the temporal cycle, which is seen, for instance, in the law that during the time of Lent no feast of a saint could be celebrated. Of course, no Sunday would ever yield to the feast of a saint, however famous.

During the Middle Ages the Sunday, besides still being the commemoration of the Resurrection of Christ, took on a special character as a day of forgiveness and mercy. From the ninth century on, the Church asked that on Sunday all military operations be suspended!

In this period falls the development of the liturgical drama. The reading of the Gospel, the reading of the Passion on Good Friday and of the Gospel of the Resurrection on Easter Sunday started it. Several members of the clergy, dressed in alb and stole, took on the different parts in order to make Holy Mass more interesting to the faithful who no longer understood Latin, the language of the Church. It became more and more common to enact parts of the Gospel stories in the sanctuary. In those times the people began to forget that the liturgy should, first and foremost, be prayer and adoration, and not entertainment for the faithful. Furthermore, throughout the Middle Ages the liturgy of the saints grew in importance. The feast of the saints were multiplying and encroaching on the Sundays. Finally, the slightest double feast had precedence over the Sunday, until, finally, in the eighteenth century only Easter Sunday and Pentecost Sunday were properly Sundays and not a saint's day. All the other liturgical Sunday Masses had vanished, even those of the Sundays of Advent and Lent. This condition lasted until, finally, the holy Pope Pius X saw the seriousness of this state of affairs and remedied it with his great reform, which gave the lost Sunday back to the Church.

This is only a brief summary of what we learned in weeks and months about the history of the Sunday. We were also made aware that Our Lord had singled out Sundays for His most solemn acts and commands—His Resurrection, the command to the Apostles to go and preach to the whole world, the institution of the Sacrament of Penance and the Descent of the Holy Ghost on Pentecost. Having realized this, the Sunday can never be a day like any other to us. It is truly a consecrated day, a day of grace.

And this launched us on a new search—for more and more knowledge about the "day of grace." From the very beginning Sunday brought to all Christians, first of all, the grace of dedication. It gave and gives them the unique chance to surrender themselves entirely to God. To what an extent this was true we came to see especially at the times of persecution. Since, from the very beginning, to assist at Mass was identical with receiving Communion, anybody who did not appear at Sunday Mass thereby excommunicated himself and was not considered a member of the Church any more. To the ones who cooperated with this grace of dedication, however, Sunday turned immediately into a day of joy, because joy is the result of dedication. As soon as we surrender ourselves completely to God, our hearts will be filled with peace and joy. Therefore, every Sunday the Church repeats in the Office the words which sound like an echo from Easter: "This is the day which the Lord hath made. Let us rejoice and be glad." So we see that, besides the grace of dedication, the liturgy of the Sunday obtains also for us the grace of joy and the grace of peace.

Another grace we discovered, which is designed directly for the majority of the faithful who cannot afford to say with the psalmist, "Seven times a day I have given praise to Thee," and for whom the seven canonical hours and the nightly vigils are some kind of spiritual luxury. God, in His great mercy, has set aside for them every week a sacred day and for that day has provided the grace of contemplation, which otherwise seems reserved only for the ones who have "time to pray." Since the days of St. Jerome it has been believed that the Sunday bestows on all who celebrate it in a Christian manner the grace of contemplation. In the Middle Ages the lay people used to flock into the convents and monasteries on Sundays to talk about God and spiritual things with the ones they considered professionals—the monks and nuns—as we can read in the autobiography of St. Teresa of Avila.

Yet another grace Sunday has in store for us. As we have a right to believe eternity will be one uninterrupted Easter Sunday, so every Sunday throughout the year helps the Christian people to prepare for that great Sunday to come. It is a day of expectation, a weekly reminder that here is only the beginning of true happiness.

The theme is endless. More and more graces will be discovered as we meditate together on the mystery of the Sunday.

It is wonderful to make such discoveries together with children or young people. To them, things are either right or wrong, and as soon as they feel in their own lives that they are not as they should be, they immediately undertake "to do something about it." That is the way it was with our children and the Sunday.

Soon after our research had begun, they founded an "Association for the Restoration of the Sunday" with Father Joseph as president. It was their own idea. The association appointed one member of the family for each Sunday, and he or she had the responsibility of seeing to it that this Sunday would be observed to the best of our ability as the Day of the Lord. The more we learned about the great sanctity of this day, the more disturbed the children became over the inadequacy of our Sunday habits. From now on, Saturday evening would be kept free from any outside appointments. The *Feierabend* would no longer be kept because "everybody did it," but because Saturday night had now become the vigil of the Day of the Lord, hallowed by almost two thousand years of observance. The Sunday clothes were no longer "an old Austrian custom." They helped to stress the sacred character of the day. No one would have wanted to put on dirty work clothes in order to take one's bicycle apart.

Even the younger ones knew that "to visit the sick" and "to help the poor" on Sunday corresponds to the character of a day of mercy —"dating back to the ninth century," they would proudly explain to an unsuspecting uncle.

But, most of all and above all, the gay, joyful character of Sunday was jealously guarded, "because this is the day we should rejoice in the Lord." The children would arrange folk dances with their friends, ball games in our garden, hikes through the mountains, and home music. Through all these activities, however, the contemplative character of Sunday was always evident, with the children demanding to read the Gospels together and to discuss the liturgy even during mealtime.

After our talk with Father Joseph, our previous observation of Sunday seemed to me like a house built on unprepared ground, until a true builder saw it, straightened it up, and put a strong foundation underneath.

And then we came to America.

In the first weeks we were too bewildered by too many things to notice any particular difference about the Sunday, but I remember missing the sound of the church bells. When I asked why the bells of St. Patrick's Cathedral do not ring on Sunday morning, I was told, to my boundless astonishment, that it would be too much noise. These were the days when the elevated was still thundering above Sixth Avenue. Never before had we heard noise like this in the heart of a city!

Then we went on our first concert tour. As we were driving from coast to coast in the big blue bus, we tried to make the most of Sunday—as much as the situation permitted. On Saturday afternoon *Feierabend* was declared, and this meant no school (our children had their lessons in the bus and had to take tests twice a year). Then we met to prepare for Mass, as had become our custom under Father Joseph. Everyone took his missal and we either crowded together in the middle of the bus or met in a hotel room, all taking turns reading the texts of the Sunday Mass. This was followed by a more or less lively discussion and a question period led by Father Wasner. Sunday we would wear our Sunday dress, the special Austrian costume set apart for that day. But otherwise Sunday was the day when we were, perhaps, a little more homesick than on any other day, missing the church bells, missing the old-world Sunday.

As we got more used to being in America and as our English progressed, we made a startling discovery: Saturday night in America! It was so utterly different from what we were used to. Everybody seemed to be out. The stores were open until ten, and people went shopping. Practically everybody seemed to go to a show or a dance or a party on Saturday night. And finally we discovered the consequence of the American Saturday night: the American Sunday morning. Towns abandoned, streets empty, everybody sleeping until the last minute and then whizzing in his car around the corner to the eleven o'clock Sunday service.

Once we were driving on a Sunday morning through the country-side in the State of Washington and we saw trucks and cars lined up along the fields and people picking berries just as on any other day. To see the farmers working on a Sunday all across the country is not unusual to us any more, and this happens not only during the most pressing seasons for crops.

When we lived in a suburb of Philadelphia in our second year in this country, we found that the rich man's Sunday delight seemed to consist of putting on his oldest torn pants and cutting his front lawn, or washing his car with a hose, or even cutting down a tree (doctor's orders—exercise!); while the ladies could be seen in dirty blue jeans mixing dirt and transplanting their perennials. There was none of that serenity and peace of the old-world Sunday anywhere until we discovered the Mennonites and the Pennsylvania Dutch. They even rang the church bells!

The climax of our discoveries about the American Sunday was reached when a lady exclaimed to us with real feeling, "Oh, how I hate Sunday! What a bore!" I can still hear the shocked silence that followed this remark. The children looked hurt and outraged, almost as if they expected fire to rain from heaven. Even the offender noticed something, and that made her explain why she hated Sunday as vigorously as she did. It explained a great deal of the mystery of the American Sunday.

"Why," she burst out, "I was brought up the Puritan way. Every Saturday night our mother used to collect all our toys and lock them up. On Sunday morning we children had to sit through a long sermon which we didn't understand; we were not allowed to jump or run or play." When she met the unbelieving eyes of our children, she repeated, "Yes, honestly—no play at all." Finally one of ours asked, "But what were you allowed to do?"

"We could sit on the front porch with the grownups or read the

Bible. That was the only book allowed on Sunday." And she added: "Oh, how I hated Sunday when I was young. I vowed to myself that when I grew up I would do the dirtiest work on Sunday, and if I should have children, they would be allowed to do exactly as they pleased. They wouldn't even have to go to church."

This was the answer. The pendulum had swung out too far to one side, and now it was going just as far in the other direction; let us hope it will find its proper position soon.

And then we bought cheaply a big, run-down farm in northern Vermont and set up home. By and by we built a house large enough for a big family, and a chapel with a little steeple and a bell. We could celebrate Sunday again to our heart's content just as we were used to doing. Saturday is a day of cleaning and cooking in our home, and five o'clock rings in *Feierabend*, when all work ceases and everyone goes to wash up and dress. If there are any guests around the supper table, Father Wasner will announce that "after the dishes are done we will all meet in the living room, everybody with his missal, for the Sunday preparation, and everyone is heartily invited to join." When we are all assembled, we start with a short prayer and then we take turns reading the different texts of the coming Sunday's Mass, everybody participating in a careful examination of these texts. First we discuss briefly the particular season of the Church year. Then we ask ourselves how this Sunday fits into the season. Do the texts suggest a special mood? Some Sundays could almost be named the Sunday of Joy, or the Sunday of Confidence, the Sunday of Humility, the Sunday of Repentance. Everybody is supposed to speak up, to ask questions, to give his opinion. It is almost always a lively, delightful discussion. At the end we determine the special message of this Sunday and what we could do during the next week to put it into action, both for ourselves and for the people around us. After this preparation for Mass, we all go into the chapel, where we say the rosary together, followed by evening prayers and Benediction.

On Sunday we often sing a High Mass, either in our chapel or in the village church, and on the big Sundays of the year we sing vespers in the afternoon. We know this should become an indispensable part of Sunday, now even more so because the Holy Father has spoken.

I remember my astonishment when our Holy Father, Pope Pius XII, found it necessary to say, in his address on Catholic Action in September, 1947: "Sunday must become again the day of the Lord, the day of adoration, of prayer, of rest, of recollection and of reflection, of happy reunion in the intimate circle of the family." Such a pronouncement, I knew, is meant for the whole world. Was Sunday endangered everywhere, then?

In the year 1950 we travelled through Mexico, Guatemala, Panama, through the Caribbean Islands and Venezuela, through Brazil and Argentina; we crossed the Andes into Chile, we gave concerts in Ecuador, Peru, and Colombia; and after many months of travel in South America, we went to Europe on a concert tour and sang in many European countries. And I came to understand that the Christian Sunday is threatened more and more both from without and from within—from without through the systematic efforts of the enemies of Christianity, and from within through the mediocrity and superficiality of the Christians themselves who are making of Sunday merely a day of rest, relaxing from work only by seeking entertainment. There was once a time, the Old Testament tells us, when people had become so lazy that they shunned any kind of spiritual effort and no longer attended public worship, so that God threatened them through the mouth of the prophet Osee: "I shall cause all her joy to cease, her feast days and her Sabbath, and all her solemn feasts."

And now the words of our present Holy Father in his encyclical "Mediator Dei" sound a similar warning:

> How will those Christians not fear spiritual death whose rest on Sundays and feast days is not devoted to religion and piety, but given over to the allurements of the world! Sundays and holidays must be made holy by divine worship which gives homage to God and heavenly food to the soul. . . . Our soul is filled with the greatest grief when we see how the Christian people profane the afternoon of feast days. . . ."

Newspapers and magazines nowadays all stress the necessity of fighting Communism. There is one weapon, however, which they do not mention and which would be the most effective one if wielded by every Christian. Again the Holy Father reminds us of it: "The results of the struggle between belief and unbelief will depend to a great extent on the use that each of the opposing fronts will make of Sunday." We know what use Russia made of the Sunday. The question now is:

And how about us—you and I?

Celebrating
with the
Family on Earth

As the Evenings Grow Longer

SOON after our first concert tour in this country letters came pouring in, always asking the same question: "What did you do to keep your family together?" or "What did you do to keep your children at home?" In answering the same question over and over again I developed something almost like a slogan, which I finally stated on the stage at every concert when giving a little introduction to our ancient instruments: "If a family plays together, sings together, and prays together—it usually stays together." In the letters I also used to say, "If you spend the first ten years with your children, they will spend the next ten years with you."

Then harassed parents wrote back asking what they should do to keep their young ones at home. They would much rather go to the movies or to a ball game. I tried to answer this at length, but to do it in writing was not very satisfactory.

Therefore, when we decided to open a summer camp—The Trapp Family Music Camp—I was delighted to be given the opportunity to show people *by doing* what we meant. The evenings of each camp session were always devoted to "home entertainment." And once the camp closes at the end of August, our home remains open for guests, and there we carry right on, living as we had been used to in Austria. In Advent we have our Advent wreath and we follow all the old customs for Advent and Christmas. We celebrate a gay Carnival and a strict Lent. We paint our Easter eggs in different ways and have as beautiful a Corpus Christi procession as we can arrange.

Every Saturday night we have our preparation for Mass—and anyone who happens to be in the house is invited to participate.

It happens quite frequently that we talk with other parents about home life. The chief regret is that entertainment has become so predominantly passive in our days. People just sit back and let themselves be entertained by watching a ball game, or television, or a movie, or listening to the radio. Almost invariably the question will be asked, "But what else could you do?"

We can only tell them what we, the Trapp family, do. Or, even better, invite them to share our evenings with us. . . .

DANCING

Coming from Austria to America meant coming from a country known from time immemorial as "the land of dancers and fiddlers," a country that had brought forth not only hundreds of most picturesque folk dances, but also that world-wide favorite, the Viennese waltz—to the country that had given to the world jazz music and the dancing that goes with it. Needless to say, we soon found ourselves engulfed in endless discussions on the subject of folk dancing versus modern ballroom dancing.

Many times we were told: "But is not jazz America's popular music and a true 'folk dance'?"

Here is my answer: Most of the so-called popular music of America certainly does not come from the people. Rather, far removed from any creative contact with this earth of ours, it is composed in some New York skyscraper; it is propagated by modern means of mass propaganda, radio and television, to a nation of one hundred and sixty millions; and upon the appearance of its successor, completely forgotten and lost.

And now let us take a look at the people who dance in the bars and nightclubs and dance halls. In the first part of the evening there prevails an air of sophistication which shows in facial expressions of bored indifference. As the evening progresses, however, the low rumbling of the rhythm seems to increase and to win out over the poverty of the melodies. And then something like a trance takes hold of the dancers as they trip around and slur and wiggle, hypnotized by the suggestive sound of the jazz orchestra.

As one looks down from a gallery on one of the modern dance halls, one is struck by something else—a picture of utter chaos. There is no pattern of movement relating the dancing couples; each pair seems alone on its narrow piece of floor, busy only with itself, with no thought for the others. The red or purple twilight mercifully conceals what could easily be read on the dancers' faces; for we must not forget that the dance is a universal language, just like music; as it involves the whole body, it has a depth and wealth of expression which surpasses by far the language of words.

It is high time for all Christian parents to wake up and see what has become of modern ballroom dancing. I say on purpose *ballroom* dancing. At the time when I was quite young, or when our mothers "came out," there existed ballroom dancing too, as distinct from folk dancing. But at that time the waltz, the minuet, the Rhinelander and polka, the quadrille, gallop, and mazurka held the place taken today by jazz and jitterbug. Each nation added one or two favorite national dances, Austria the "Laendler," Sweden the "Hombo," Jugoslavia the "Kolo," Hungaria the "Czardas." How could one single generation have been so careless as to lose all these precious goods which had enriched the lives of many generations?

The last years, however, seem to have brought about a reaction. In French Canada there is the beginning of a movement aimed to reintroduce folk dancing to young people. In America the English and Irish square dances are becoming increasingly popular, and all over the country little groups seriously interested in the folk dances of many nations are forming. We were surprised to find on the West Coast even more interest in folk dancing than in the East.

We have always enjoyed our inheritance of Austrian folk dances. As we started touring all over Europe we exchanged our own national dances for those of the country whose guests we were. So it comes that we have a large collection of European folk dances which we brought home from our travels. From the very beginning of our summer Music Camp, folk dancing has been an integral part of our evening entertainment. It was always a joy and a rewarding happiness to see how everybody took to it enthusiastically.

One difficulty is usually the music. One should realize from the very beginning that record players are not the right accompaniment for folk dancing. They are too mechanical, too rigid. People simply have to learn to play instruments again: accordion and guitar, fiddle and clarinet, or the recorder, the ancient flute that is gaining so many new friends today.

One thing is sure: people have always danced, and always will. By experience we have learned that it is not enough to criticize an existing system; one should rather supplant it with a better one, overcome the evil with the good. Parents might get interested in the nearest folk dancing group, join in their evenings, learn the dances, read about them, learn to play the dances on simple instruments and then introduce them in their own homes. With these folk dances, old and new, and the ballroom dances of our own youth, we shall be able to enjoy many a happy evening together with our families.

One more thing needs to be said here: there are times when dancing is allowed and times when dancing is forbidden: "All things have their season. . . . There is a time to weep and a time to laugh, a time to mourn, and a time to dance" (Ecclesiastes 2:1-4). This also has become forgotten, and dances in parish halls on Saturday evenings during Advent and Lent are not infrequent. Again, we have to wake up from our sleep, or shall we call it stupor, and look to our Christian inheritance in order to learn when we should dance and when not. Then, in spite of "but everybody does it," we shall act accordingly. It may not always be easy to be a true Christian, but it brings inner happiness—that kind of happiness which is the result of a sacrifice cheerfully brought—the happiness the children of the world ignore.

READING ALOUD

One of our favorite evening pastimes has always been reading aloud. In the old country, when I could do it in German, I would read what amounted eventually to a small library, while the family would be knitting, darning, or whittling. Among the books were historical novels, which led quite naturally into talking and discussing the period of that time; short stories; and one or the other of the great novels of world literature. Stevenson's *Treasure Island*, Kipling's *Kim* and, of course, his *Mowgli* Stories delighted the younger listeners. Such readings would go on over several weeks; we would hurry from supper into the library and settle around the fireplace for a few hours' intense enjoyment of one of the world's literary masterpieces. (In this way a great many Christmas gifts got finished, too.)

Then we discovered the great pleasure of reading plays together, each one reading a part aloud. Some of Shakespeare's tragedies and comedies should be read this way in every home.

If the children are led by stages from the fairy-tale age to *Winnie the Pooh, Little Women, Oliver Twist*—to mention but a few of the childhood classics—they will come to demand another such session every winter. In later years they will refer to those times as: "the winter we were reading *Great Expectations*" or "that winter when we were plowing through *War and Peace*."

Quite apart from acquainting us with the best works of the world's great writers, it cannot be stressed enough that reading as a group is altogether different from reading for oneself. Family reading provides another valuable thing in great danger of dropping out of our lives—the ability to form an opinion and state it—which is the very essence of group discussion. As the children grow up, the books will change in character. There will be biographies of saints, books on the spiritual life, and books of philosophical character. The discussions that grow quite naturally from our readings may later belong to our children's most cherished memories.

GROUP DISCUSSION

Once, in one of our camp seasons, a lady said to me just before lunch, "Can't we have a discussion some day?" I answered quickly, "Oh, certainly—on what?" and was slightly baffled when she answered cheerily, "Never mind on what—just a discussion." This led me to announce at the end of lunch: "At three o'clock we shall have a discussion. Everybody who is interested please come to Stephen Foster Hall." Everybody was at Stephen Foster Hall at three o'clock, wondering what the discussion would be about. I started out by relating the little incident before lunch and inviting those present to name a few topics which might be of general interest. And we had a most enjoyable hour. The topic finally was: "What can we—the ones who are present—contribute toward world peace?" I remember the keen interest of the whole group—how they listened to a grade school teacher, a dentist, a country doctor, a nurse, several housewives, a grandmother, a university professor, a factory worker, a missionary from China. . . . Ever since that experience we have such a discussion meeting—the topic chosen by those present—in each Sing Week at least once.

Occasionally we also spend an evening or a Sunday afternoon at home in our bay window discussing old or new questions, such as "What is beautiful?" (still not settled though much pondered and discussed with many different groups of friends and members of the family). Modern art is another widely, and wildly, discussed subject, with special emphasis, in our house, on modern music. "The Time of the Gadget," as I disrespectfully refer to the technical age, is also hotly discussed.

Some of these discussions come about quite naturally, some of them could be planned. In this way growing children learn not only to listen to and to respect another's opinion, but also to state their own bravely, even if it should be opposed by the rest of the group. Do not the Gospels show us Our Lord, ever so often, involved in discussions with His friends, the Apostles, or holding His own against His enemies, the Pharisees!

SINGING

From the very time when the first baby is born, the mother should sing to her child. There are innumerable lullabies, nursery rhymes, and little prayers to be found in songbooks, just waiting to be brought to life. Parents will be astonished at how soon the little ones will carry a tune, and this will lead naturally to singing in parts, with

Mummy taking over the second and Daddy later adding the third. Singing is something entirely natural. If only one could cure that horrible phobia we come across so often: "I can't sing—I don't have a piano!" The most beautiful instrument is the human voice, which God gave to everyone.

The radio could provide a valuable education in every household if listening were planned intelligently with the help of the weekly program. But often the radio is turned on early in the morning, to be turned off only after the lights are put out at night. More than once when people invited us to their homes after a concert, I noticed that even before they switched on the light they turned the knob on the radio. It always filled me with awe to see how completely this piece of machinery dominates our homes. Let's turn off the radio so that we may discover our own voices in an evening of song.

From years of experience here in America we know how much fun everybody gets out of singing "rounds"; so let us begin by singing every round first in unison; and when everyone knows the melody well enough to hold his own, in two parts; and later, in three or four —whatever this particular round calls for.

"Rounds" are performed in the following way: One singer, or one group of singers, starts out. When the score shows the figure "2," the second singer, or second group, comes in, and so on. One can end rounds in two different ways: (1) Either everyone keeps on singing the melody and repeating it until the leader indicates the time to end and the singers hold the tone marked by ⌒. (In the notation of rounds this is what ⌒ stands for.) (2) Or a round may be ended in the same manner it began: by having every part sing their melody twice or three times and then stop, so that the last group to start singing is the last to finish. Most of the time you can use any combination of equal or unequal voices for the singing of rounds. Very soon you will hear these rounds sung throughout the house during dishwashing, during housework—wherever there are two or more people in the same room—or in summer while weeding in the garden. Singing rounds is the most natural and easiest way to school the ear for part singing. Here we give a few songs from our summer program which have become favorites in many an American home.

WELCOME, WELCOME!

Published in 1849 in Nashville, Tenn., by W. Walker. The
FOUR PARTS "Sacred Nine" in the text are the Nine Muses.

1. Welcome, welcome ev'-ry guest, welcome to our mu-sic fest,

2. Mu-sic is our plea-sant cheer, fills both soul and ra-vished ear.

3. Sa-cred Nine teach us thy mood, sweetest notes to be ex-plored.

4. Soft-ly fill the eve-ning air, to complete our concert fair!

SI CANTEMO

Antonio Caldara, 1670-1736.

THREE PARTS

1. Si can-te - mo la la la co-sì l'o-re ne pas-se-rà.

2. La la la, la la la la, la la la la ne pas-se - rà.

3. La la la, la la la, la la ne pas-se- rà.

THE NIGHTINGALE

Pammelia: Musicks Miscellanie, Or, Mixed Varietie of Pleasant

THREE PARTS   *Roundelayes, London, 1609.*

The nightingale, the merry nightingale, she sweet-ly sits and sings and sings. The pretty nimble doe doth trip it to and fro, the wild horse kicks and flings and flings. The cu - ckoo he doth fly from tree to tree, and merri-ly through the woods cuckoo, cuckoo sings.

THE MUSICIANS

TWO PARTS   Anonymous.

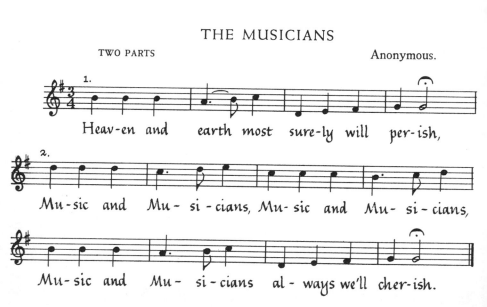

Heav-en and earth most sure-ly will per-ish,

Mu-sic and Mu - si - cians, Mu- sic and Mu - si - cians,

Mu-sic and Mu - si - cians al - ways we'll cher-ish.

THREE GEESE ARE SITTING NEAR

FOUR PARTS   Anonymous.

1. Three geese are sit-ting near in a barn and without fear.

2. See the far-mer's com - ing with a big stick loom - ing,

3. cries out: Who's here, who's here, who's here?

4. Three —— geese are sit - ting near.

QUANDO CONVENIUNT (GOSSIP CANON)

Anonymous. Sing this round as fast as you are able, let every part sing the melody twice and then end. Where there are enough people, a charming effect may be obtained by doubling male and female voices in every part. Do not forget the dynamic contrast between the first and the second line!

FOUR PARTS

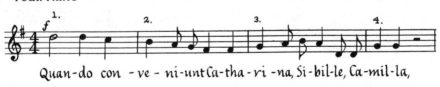

Quan-do con - ve - ni-unt Ca-tha-ri -na, Si-bil-le, Ca-mil-la,

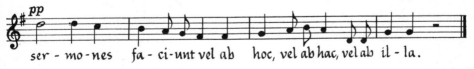

ser - mo - nes fa - ci-unt vel ab hoc, vel ab hac, vel ab il - la.

IF I KNEW

THREE PARTS

Franz Lachner, 1803-1890.

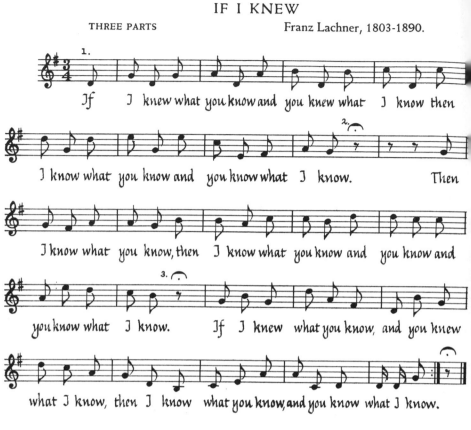

If I knew what you know and you knew what I know then
I know what you know and you know what I know. Then
I know what you know, then I know what you know and you know and
you know what I know. If I knew what you know, and you knew
what I know, then I know what you know, and you know what I know.

DEATH AND SLEEP

FOUR PARTS

J. Haydn.

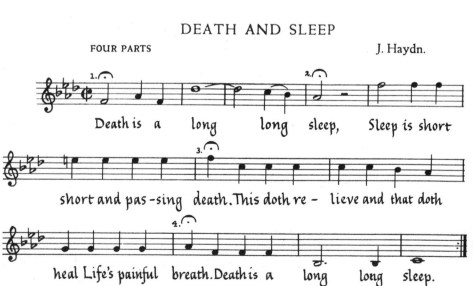

Death is a long long sleep, Sleep is short
short and pas-sing death. This doth re - lieve and that doth
heal Life's painful breath. Death is a long long sleep.

THE WISE MEN

THREE PARTS   William Lawes, 1602-1645.

1. The Wise Men were but sev'n, ne'er more shall be for
2. The Vir-tues they are sev'n. And three the great-er

1. me ——: The Mus-es were but nine, the
2. be ——: The Cae-sars they were twelve And the

1. Worthies three times three. And three mer-ry boys and
2. Fa-tal Sis-ters three: And three mer-ry girls and

1. three merry boys, and three merry boys are we.
2. three merry girls, and three merry girls are we.

THE ST. MARTIN'S CANON

Anonymous, 14th century. From a manuscript of the Monastery
THREE PARTS   in Lambach. Austria.

Martin, dearest Mas-ter, now let us all be

gay! We would do you ho-nor on this your fes-tal

day. The geese are fat and ten-der, sweet and cool the

wine. We'll boil them and we'll fry them and on them richly dine.

NEW OYSTERS

Three English Street-Cries combined to a Round. From *Pammelia*, 1609.

THREE PARTS

VIVA LA MUSICA!

THREE PARTS　　　　　Michael Praetorius, 1571-1621.

II.

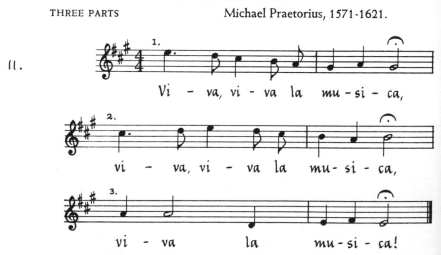

SING HEAVE AND HO

William Byrd, called the "Father of English Music," 1543-1623.

Hey ho ——, to the green-wood now let us go, sing
heave and ho, and there shall we find both buck and
doe, sing heave and ho, the hart and hind and the
little pret — ty roe, sing heave and ho.

COME, FOLLOW

THREE PARTS   John Hilton, 1599-1657.

Come fol-low, fol-low, fol-low, fol-low, fol-low,
fol-low me! Wither shall I fol-low, fol-low, fol-low,
wither shall I fol-low, fol-low Thee? To the green-wood,
to the greenwood, to the green-wood, green-wood tree!

FLOW GENTLY, SWEET AFTON

Text, Robert Burns (1786). Melody, Alexander Hume.

If third part is sung by a male voice, read an octave higher.

1. Flow gent-ly sweet Af-ton, a - mong thy green braes; Flow
2. Thy crystal stream Af-ton, how love-ly it glides, And

1. gent-ly, I'll sing thee a song in thy praise; My
2. winds by the cot where my Ma-ry re - sides. How

1. Ma - ry's a - sleep by thy mur-mur-ing stream, Flow
2. wan-ton thy wa - ters her snow-y feet lave, As

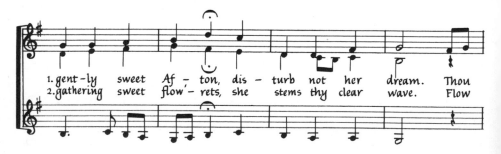

1. gent-ly sweet Af - ton, dis - turb not her dream. Thou
2. gathering sweet flow'-rets, she stems thy clear wave. Flow

1. stock-dove, whose e-cho re-sounds from the hill, Ye
2. gent-ly sweet Af-ton, a-mong thy green braes, Flow

1. wild whis-tling black-birds in yon thorn-y dell, Thou
2. gent-ly, sweet riv-er, the theme of my lays; My

1. green crest-ed lap-wing, thy screaming for-bear, I
2. Ma-ry's a-sleep by thy mur-mur-ing stream, Flow

1. charge you dis-turb not my slum-ber-ing fair.
2. gent-ly, sweet Af-ton, dis-turb not her dream.

THE ECHO

SIX PARTS

Padre Martini, 1706-1784.

Ho, through the forest hear the e-cho ring! Back it
an-swers: Tra la la la la la, tra la la, tra la la.

DONA NOBIS PACEM

THREE PARTS

Anonymous.

Do - na no - bis pa — cem, pa-cem,
do — na no - bis pa — cem. Do -
na no - bis pa-cem, do - na no - bis
pa — cem. Do - na no - bis
pa-cem, do - na no - bis pa — cem.

WHY DOES LIFE

THREE PARTS. ANDANTE   Antonio Caldara, 1670-1736.

Why does life bring me no-thing but sorrow,
Since I have met you O sweetheart mine? When I am
near you, love does tor-ment me, Far from your presence there's
naught but pain. When I am near you, love does tor-
ment me, Far from your pre-sence there's naught but pain.

GOOD NIGHT

THREE PARTS. ANDANTE E LEGATO   American Round.

Good night to you all and sweet be your sleep!
May si-lence sur-round you, your slum-ber be deep!
Good night, good night, good night, good night!

HOME CONCERTS

What we said about sharing the masterpieces in world literature through family reading should be said with equal emphasis for the listening to the masterpieces of the world's music. Young married couples might find among their wedding gifts a stock of long-playing records—since "hi-fi" brings Carnegie Hall not only to every town, but practically into every home!

As the children grow up, they will get used to being cautioned to silence while father and mother are listening to some symphony, opera, or vocal concert on the record player. A well-stocked record library makes it easy for us to arrange for a real concert on Saturday nights (when we don't go out!) or Sunday afternoons, or special feast-day evenings around the year.

The great oratorios cannot be listened to in one sitting, and understood and enjoyed at the same time. One section should be played at a time and played more than once, until the listener grows familiar with each part and learns to appreciate the whole work. The weeks of Advent are an excellent period for a study of "The Messiah," and the weeks of Lent for the "St. Matthew Passion"; then, at the end of the season, at Christmas and during Holy Week, the entire work will be played in one sitting.

For the Christmas season, there are the Christmas carols by the Robert Shaw Chorale; the Christmas music of early Italian composers, played by I *Virtuosi di Roma,* or the two records "Christmas with the Trapp Family." Lent might be the time for Negro spirituals, for the oratorio (for example, "The Seven Last Words" by Haydn or the "German Requiem" of Brahms) or for Mozart's Great Mass in C Minor.

We have had considerable experience with people who viewed our selection of records with great suspicion and when exposed to such a "concert at home," were preparing themselves to be "bored to death with that long-haired music," only to exclaim afterwards, "But that is beautiful!"

For those who want to start the experiment, here are four works

which are so captivating, even to the untrained ear, that everybody
without exception has enjoyed them at first hearing:

> Mozart, Quintet for Clarinet & Strings in A Major, K. 581
> Mozart, Quartet for Oboe & Strings
> Mozart, "Eine kleine Nachtmusik"
> Haydn, Concerto for Trumpet & Orchestra in D Major

Here are some program suggestions for such "Concerts at Home,"
which of course each family will vary to suit its tastes:

> Respighi, "Suite of Ancient Arias and Dances"
> Mozart, Symphony in D Major ("Prague")
>
>   *   *   *
>
> Bach, Brandenburg Concerto I in F Major
> Schubert, Quintet for Strings in C Major, op. 163
>   (one of the most moving, most beautiful works of all time)
>
>   *   *   *
>
> Mozart, "Eine kleine Nachtmusik"
> Schubert, Symphony No. 8 in B Minor ("Unfinished")
>
>   *   *   *
>
> Mozart, Serenade in E Flat Major
> Schubert, Symphony No. 7 in C Major ("Great")

The prejudice so many have against operas could easily be overcome by first getting acquainted with their texts. For a few cents one
can get *The Pocket Book of Great Operas* by Henry W. Simon and
Abraham Veinus, (Pocket Books, Inc., New York, 1949). There one
can find the story of the most popular operas, and that is the first
gate to cross. Then we suggest that you listen to one act at a time,
and read first the story (which nearly every album includes with the
records) and then the libretto, following the original text and translation until you are thoroughly familiar with it and can enjoy the
whole without a book or translation.

Operas suggested for family enjoyment are Mozart's *The Magic
Flute*, Wagner's *Die Meistersinger*, Verdi's *Aida*; and the children in
particular will delight in Humperdinck's *Hänsel and Gretel* and
Menotti's *Amahl and the Night Visitors*, which is especially appropriate for the Christmas season.

If you wish to end such an evening on a lighter vein, add one of the great waltzes by Johann Strauss in the authentic, wonderful performance of the Vienna Philharmonic Orchestra.

"ONCE UPON A TIME"

Among the arts that are dying out rapidly in our machine age, the one most in danger is the art of story-telling. In other generations it was quite natural that every mother would tell her little ones a story at bed-time, or when a child didn't feel well, or on Sundays and feast days. Those were the times when mothers were really busy, when they had to light a fire in the kitchen stove, to wash their laundry by hand, to shop every morning and carry their marketing home—sometimes over long distances—when they were sewing the children's clothes and mending and darning in the evening. But there was always time left to tell a story.

There is no substitute for story-telling. The reading of books, privately or aloud, the listening to radio and watching television—all these devices cannot replace one single, live story told around the fireplace or on the front porch on a summer night, or after the bonfire has died down.

Admittedly, it is not an easy art. Many people have found that out and have given up before trying hard enough.

A lot of story-telling has gone on in our house. My husband was a master of it. When he started to tell about his trip around the world in an old-fashioned frigate as a cadet first class, or of his participation in the Boxer Rebellion in China when he was nineteen, or of his adventures in the first newly invented, poorly constructed submarines, we all would sit spellbound, oblivious of time.

Once we spent a delightful summer with Robert Flaherty and his family. He was another master of this forgotten art. Almost every night, on the lawn in front of his Vermont home, he told about his experiences with the Eskimos, or with the South Sea people—again banishing time.

One is always sure of captivating an audience with ghost stories. There are plenty of true ghost stories—one just has to look for them

—true because they might tell of an experience with the world beyond.

It isn't so much what we tell—as long as we are willing to revive this forgotten art. Our Lord gives us an example. Some of the most beautiful stories ever told come from Him—the story of the Prodigal Son, of Lazarus, of the Good Samaritan.

And now we have reached the most important point of all. When sermons or devotional books tell us that the Christian family should fashion itself on the example of the Holy Family, this usually refers to the spiritual life only. "If there were more mothers like Mary and more fathers like Joseph, there would be more children like Jesus," it is said, Mary being thought of as the holy handmaid of the Lord, Joseph as the man nearest to God, and the Infant "subject unto them." Nowhere have I seen that thought extended to the whole of our family life, calling us to model our recreations, also, on the example of the Holy Family. It is not at all likely that Jesus, Mary, and Joseph would have gone to some of the shows in our movie theatres or into any one of our night clubs or the average Broadway show. It is quite probable, however, that there was story-telling, singing, and discussion going on in the evenings in the little house in Nazareth; and why shouldn't they have played games with the little Boy and His friends, or listened to music played on the quaint ancient instruments by some neighbors? Joseph may have read to his family, and whenever they accepted an invitation to a wedding of one of their kinfolk, they certainly participated in the solemn dancing which formed part of any oriental wedding ceremony.

A word from the Book of Wisdom is often applied to Our Lord or to His Holy Mother: "My joy it is to be with the children of men." Should we limit this "togetherness" to one hasty half-hour on Sundays, from eleven to eleven-thirty? Knowing that it means such joy for them, let us invite the Holy Family to stay with us throughout the days of the week, throughout the years of our life: when we work or pray, and also when we play.

Our Life—A Feast

EVERYTHING from booklets to tomes is being written, in alarmingly increasing numbers, on one topic: the deterioration of family life and what to do about it. As one looks over those more or less learned treatises, however, one misses one phrase—*family feasts*—and yet that makes all the difference. Why have homes more and more turned into places where a group of people merely happen to live under one roof, each member going his separate way, sharing nothing with the others? The answer is that they lack family feasts.

Holy Mother Church knows that in all families, no matter how seriously they strive for perfection, how honestly they all want to become saints, there are times when parents or children alike may lose their temper, may give way to selfishness or possessiveness, when the mother makes imprudent judgments, children give in to self-pity, and everybody gets fed up. That may, and does, happen to all of us. Why? Because we are all created alike. We have inherited original sin and we suffer from the scars of the old wound. But the Church has given us the feast and has taught us how to celebrate, and it is the hallmark of a feast that it cannot be celebrated by a solitary individual. There has to be a group. It is the feast that helps to keep the family together.

This is true from the very beginning of family life. From the weekly celebration of the Day of the Lord, and from the yearly cycle of feasts of Christmastide and Paschaltide, the young parents have learned how to celebrate. As the children are coming along and witness how beautifully the father celebrates the feast days of the mother—her birthday, her baptismal day, the feast of her patron saint, their wedding anniversary—and when they see with how much love the mother prepares the great days of the father—then the children come to experience a feeling of security which they will need so greatly in later life—the warmth of the nest which the young bird needs before he can spread his own wings.

This is how it starts: The father draws the attention of the children to the coming feast days of the mother, and the mother does the same for the father. The older sisters and brothers teach the little ones. There is always a lot of secrecy around our house in the days before a feast, a lot of whispering and preparations behind closed doors. "Before a birthday, there's a prickle in the air like ginger ale," said one of my children once.

In order to keep a record of all the various feasts—no mean achievement in as large a family as ours—my daughter Rosemary has devised an "Anniversary Calendar," one page of which is here reproduced. (Anyone with a knack for drawing can attempt something similar as a homemade gift!)

THE BIRTHDAY

There are the birthdays. I suppose there are as many ways of celebrating a birthday as there are families, or even as there are individuals. In our family some of our children, pointing out that the big feasts in the year have a vigil, insisted that their birthday should be celebrated the evening before so that they could have the full day following in which to be the center of attention in the house. Some prefer their birthdays to be celebrated at breakfast; others, during lunch. That should be up to the individual. For days, sometimes for weeks, the preparations are going on. If everybody, as it should be, is supposed to make something for everybody else's birthday, this—and I cannot stress it enough—will bring out hidden talents in the family. We only found out by chance that one of our children is gifted in leather work, that another one makes beautiful woodcuts.

JANUARY

Nor let anxious thoughts fret
thy life away, a merry heart is
the true life of man; length of
years is measured by rejoicing
Eccu. 30,22

Date	Birthday	Feastday	Anniversary		Date	Birthday	Feastday	Anniversary
1					16			
2					17			
3					18			
4					19			
5					20			
6					21			
7					22			
8					23			
9					24			
10					25			
11					26			
12					27			
13					28			
14					29			
15					30			
					31			

One of the boys turned out to be a good silversmith, and one of the girls is working in clay. If the children are given a chance to try this or that handicraft, they are sure to discover some special gift. And the most gifted cook, of course, is entrusted with preparing the birthday cake.

In our family we have two favorite birthday cakes. Number One is that famous Viennese *Sacher Torte*.

Sacher Torte

4 oz. butter	7 eggs
4 oz. sugar	1 cup bread flour
4 oz. softened bittersweet	2 tbsp. fine bread crumbs
chocolate	

Beat butter, sugar, and softened chocolate together. Add one egg yolk at a time. Beat 7 egg whites until peaks stand up straight. Add to mixture. Then add bread flour and bread crumbs. Mix in by hand with rubber spatula. Bake slowly in well-greased, floured cake tin. When cool, cut in half horizontally. Spread apricot jam on lower half. Cover with upper half and spread evenly with apricot jam. Let dry for a while.

Icing: In upper part of double boiler melt 3 oz. bitter chocolate, 2 oz. sweet chocolate, 3 oz. butter. Add ⅓ cup of cream. Stir. Remove from heat. Add ½ box sifted confectioner's sugar. Pour icing on the torte and spread around sides with spatula.

Number Two is *Linzer Torte*.

Linzer Torte

1½ cups flour	2 tsp. cinnamon
1 cup sugar	¼ tsp. salt
2 egg yolks	½ tsp. cloves
1 tsp. baking powder	1 cup ground nuts or almonds
1 tbsp. orange or lemon peel	

Sift flour and baking powder together onto a pastry board. Add sugar, egg yolks, orange or lemon peel, nuts, cinnamon, cloves, and salt. Mix by hand and chill. Pat ⅔ of dough into layercake tin and spread with a layer of currant preserve. Roll remaining ⅓ of dough into strips as thick as a finger. With this, form a lattice work on top of preserve. Bake in medium oven 350-375 degrees F. until edges recede from sides.

Now to the celebration itself. A small table is covered with a white cloth. The birthday cake with the candles is put in the middle and the gifts are placed around it. The whole household—family, helpers, guests—stand in a semicircle, each one holding a flower or a piece of evergreen, according to the season. Then the mother goes to fetch the birthday child. "Happy Birthday to You" is sung until the hero of the day has been congratulated and kissed by everyone. In the process, he gathers his little bouquet. Then he thinks of a wish and blows out the candles (in one breath!), and then he looks at the gifts. (One of the first birthday presents, when the children were quite small, was a puppet theatre. With each birthday new puppets were added and all the favorite fairy tales could be enacted.)

The birthday child's place at table is decorated artistically—differently at each meal—and he decides what the day's and the evening's entertainment will be—games, or folk dancing, or perhaps an excursion. Whatever it is, we all are at his or her disposal.

BAPTISMAL DAY

More important than our real birthday, the anniversary of the moment when our mother gave us our physical life, is the anniversary of the moment when we received the life of our soul as children of God. Why should we not start a new tradition in our young families, following an ancient custom of the first centuries where the Christians were much more imbued with awe for that great Sacrament of

Baptism? We should start to celebrate the baptismal days of our children, to which we should invite the godparents and anyone else who had been present at the baptism of that child. If the godparents cannot come, they might be asked to write a letter each year to their godchild, thus keeping the spiritual relationship alive. In the time of our great-grandparents such letters were reverently kept through life. That's why it is so important to choose godparents who can be relied upon to take their spiritual fatherhood and motherhood seriously.

When the children are little, we should tell them of their baptismal day in the form of a story. Later, we should go with them through the ceremonies and rites of the Sacrament of Baptism. We should take them, if at all possible, back to the baptismal font and there solemnly renew with them the baptismal vows. At the end of such a day the whole family might gather and sing solemnly, "Holy God, We Praise Thy Name," or another hymn of thanksgiving.

If on birthdays all kinds of secular gifts are given, on the baptismal day we might give, gradually, all that our children require for their spiritual life: a missal, starting with a small missal for children, until they finally get the unabridged *Missale Romanum*; the New Testament; later the complete Bible; a holy water font; a crucifix; blessed candles for their little altar in their private corner. On this day, the baptismal candle should be taken out and put in a candlestick. The white garment which the child wore at his baptism and which we should keep for him should also be taken out, and the children should be reminded of the intention underlying the Church's words: "Receive this burning light and safeguard thy baptism by a blameless life. Keep the Commandments of God that when Our Lord shall come to claim His own, thou mayest be worthy to greet Him with all the saints in the heavenly court and live forever and ever. Amen.

"Receive this white garment which thou mayest wear without stain before the judgment seat of Our Lord, Jesus Christ, that thou mayest have life everlasting. Amen."

If only we would start this tradition right now, and if the godparents could be persuaded to see their role on such a day, what a beautiful, solemn and sacred day it might become in our families!

THE FEAST OF THE PATRON SAINT

Another feast day has fallen more and more into oblivion, and that is the celebration of the feast of our patron saints, in other words, our feast days. Alas, instead of choosing the names of the saints which are given to us by the Church as our patrons, as our big brothers and sisters, our protectors and intercessors—more and more people choose names of their own invention which have no relationship to Christianity. I know of one young mother who called her little daughter in honor of her own alma mater, "University of Texas"; I know another family who gave one of their boys the name of the place where they had a summer cabin; and a third one of our acquaintances called their little child, hoping it would make her a musician, "Melody."

This is a good moment for us parents to make an examination of conscience—by what principles do we choose the names of our children? Do we think of the saint, or do we think of the sound of the name, or are we persuaded by the fact that the godfather or the godmother might be offended if we didn't choose his or her name, although we really don't care much for it? It is a heavy responsibility to choose one of the greatest spiritual beings for the guidance and protection of our children.

The day of the patron saint is celebrated on a somewhat smaller scale than a birthday. The gifts have some relation to the patron saint—books, pictures, legends pertaining to him are collected throughout the years. Again the feast-day child has his own say about the evening's program.

And here let me mention a thing which cannot be sufficiently stressed: that we parents have to have enough time to play with our children. We have to know their games. The very fact that so many mothers and fathers nowadays find no time any more to join in games with their little children is the very beginning of the breakdown of modern families. In the first seven years of a child's life the child either grows away from his parents, or a strong tie is formed.

Merely by observing, one finds out that children play different games at different seasons of the year. Only in the fall do they want to run around with kites or play cops and robbers. In the spring, when they can get out after a long winter, they are on swings, climbing trees, jumping rope, and trying their skill on stilts. In the summer, obviously because of the heat, they prefer more quiet games, if possible water games and ball games; while the winter finds them around the table with checkers and dominoes, rummy, and, nowadays, scrabble, and all kinds of guessing games, until a good snowfall allows them to go out with their skis and sleds.

It is most important also for fathers to know the seasonal character of the games of the little ones. Just as the birds build their nests in the spring and start for their long flight in the fall, so it seems the children carry an old instinct and have to live accordingly. You can't make them play indoor games in spring!

All the "firsts" might be celebrated in a festive way.

For a little child, it is a big and important day when he goes, for the first time in his young life, to school. This we have turned into a family feast. The mother goes shopping for school books and all the immensely important little paraphernalia, and accompanies the child for the first time on this important trip, which marks a new chapter in its life. It is the first step towards "coming of age."

FIRST CONFESSION

Then there is the first Confession. To turn such a day into a "holy day" we parents should prepare ourselves for it by special study and much prayer in order to be able to give the child an even deeper understanding of what he is going to do when he kneels down and confesses—not to Father So-and-So, but to God, Himself—all the wrongs that cloud his young conscience. When he is going to hear for the first time the momentous words, "Thy sins are forgiven!" we help him realize with chalk and blackboard what will happen to him. We write down a list of sins such as a child may commit, and then we take a wet cloth and erase them completely and ask the child,

"Can you still read what was there? Just like this God will erase your sins from His memory. He will forgive them completely." We cannot do enough to impress the young soul with the tremendous happening at the moment of the *"Ego te absolve."* Of course, the child should remember the day of his first Confession and always later celebrate this anniversary as a private feast day just between himself and God.

FIRST HOLY COMMUNION

Then comes the great day when the young soul is for the first time invited to the heavenly banquet—the day of the first Holy Communion. It is a pity that this sacred day so often degenerates into a show, the child being showered with gifts and distracted with amusements, so that this solemn, holy feast turns into a day of much outward excitement. Again, there is much we Christian parents have to learn to do better. The preparation for this day, the first Holy Communion of our children, should be a holy rite and duty for every mother. We can learn from the family of St. Thérèse of Lisieux how the older sisters saw to it that the younger ones were prepared sufficiently for their great day. Of course, the whole family should join the child at the Communion Mass, everybody wearing his Sunday dress. Not only the table, but the house or apartment should be decorated. For the rest of his life the child will remember this day. Instead of many worthless trinkets, one might buy one real gift, either a beautiful medal or little cross to wear around the child's neck, or a picture for his room, a reproduction of the old masters, or a beautiful statue. These are formative years, and it is our privilege to school the taste of our children, directing them away from the sweetish, coy plaster art, toward genuine art.

CONFIRMATION

Another great day is the day of Confirmation, the spiritual coming of age of the young Christian. Much could we learn here from the Orthodox Jewish families and their way of celebrating the Bar-Mitzvah on the boy's thirteenth birthday, when he becomes of age before the law. The coming of the Holy Ghost, the sacrament of holy ordination for us lay people, cannot receive enough attention. It is a great joy to help the child prepare for this, his very own, Pentecost. With him we study the "Gifts of the Holy Ghost" and the "Fruits of the Holy Ghost"; we read together such books as Father Grandmaison's *We and the Holy Spirit* or the chapters pertaining to the Holy Ghost in *The Spiritual Life* by Adolphe Tanquerey; unforgettable hours are thus spent, in which we accompany our sons and daughters on their road to spiritual maturity.

We have always tried to mark the day of Confirmation by a gift or event which stresses the new status of the child as a person capable of independence and responsibility; f.i., by giving him a desk of his own, or, if possible, a room of his own. (It is significant that it is the custom to give a watch on Confirmation Day, to remind the young Christian that from now on he is responsible for the use of his time.)

These are the commanding high points in the lives of the young, and I feel that one can never do enough to make them into memorable events, keeping them alive in the memory of our children by celebrating the anniversaries of these days.

Children who have experienced the joy of being feasted will want to reciprocate. All the love and attention that is showered on them they will try to return just as lovingly and gratefully as their young hearts prompt them to do.

WEDDING ANNIVERSARY

In the first years, while the children are still very young, mother and father will celebrate the wedding anniversary by themselves. But as the children grow older, they should be allowed to participate in this great family feast—the day beginning with Holy Communion for all, followed by a feast-day breakfast. Afterwards, one might talk with them about the character of matrimony, and read with them the nuptial blessing and the blessing of the wedding ring. This implants in the young ones a deep respect for this great sacrament, and fosters a reverent attitude toward each other in the hearts of boys and girls.

EMBER DAYS

Alas, the holy seasons of the Ember Days, which recur four times a year at the beginning of spring, summer, fall and winter, are no longer observed as they were in the old Church, namely as days of ordination of our priests when the Church wants her faithful to remember her priests by prayer and sacrifice. Nowadays, we have "Priest's Saturday," which takes, somewhat, the place of those very holy seasons. Ember Saturday, which was the day of the final ordinations, is the day when we might explain the sacrament of Holy Orders to the children. On the evenings of these Saturdays, after preparation for the Mass, we could tell them about the holiness of priesthood and sisterhood, about our Holy Father, the Pope, about the cardinals and bishops, and particularly about our own bishop— our true representative of Christ. We could remind them to remember the Pope, the bishop, and all the priests in their daily prayers. If it is at all possible, we might have them participate in the yearly ordination ceremonies, a great liturgical experience.

GRADUATION DAYS

Time goes by quickly. And though it appears to us mothers as if it were only yesterday that we took our little child on his first walk to school, graduation days are fast approaching—from grade school, from high school, from college. Each one of these days we celebrate as a family feast. This gives us an opportunity to talk to our children about their future, and to try to counteract, with all the weight of our affection, the influence of the world which holds out to the young the promise of "how to earn the most money." We impress on our children the meaning of the word "vocation," which is not restricted to priesthood or the religious life. *"Vocare"* means "to call," and every person on earth is called by God to a special place where He wants him or her. It may be that of a nurse or a teacher, of a salesman, of a worker in a plant or a missionary in Africa—but there is that particular place and we have to find it. One of the main reasons why there are today so many frustrated people is that most of them never managed to discover their true place in life. But if a girl is called to be a nurse, she will be very unhappy as a secretary, even if she has a much easier life. If someone is called to be a teacher, he will never be really satisfied as a business man, no matter how successful. In revealing to the children the great mystery of the vocation, we help to prepare them to make the right choice in life. The only question in the young mind should be: What is the will of God? Where does He want me? Only by finding the place God has prepared for us will we be really efficient and happy.

EXTREME UNCTION

Among the seven sacraments there is one for which most people have lost the proper understanding—the sacrament of Extreme Unction, the great friend of all the sick. Unfortunately, it has become known as the sacrament of the dying. Out of a mistaken consideration for the sick, in order "not to excite him," he is all too often made to believe he really isn't very sick at all. When illness finally takes a turn for the worst, the poor patient is often no longer able to follow the deeply consoling prayers and rites of this great sacrament. But if it is introduced to children early in life, as one of the greatest gifts of God, there will be no fear.

All Souls' Day lends itself by its very character to a meditation

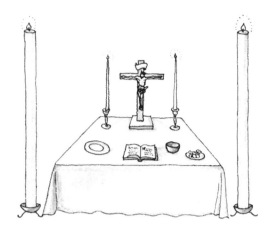

on the last things. This is the day on which we show our children
how one prepares a table for administering Extreme Unction. The
first time I do this myself, telling the children to watch carefully
as next year *they* will have to prepare it. I show them in which
drawer I keep the crucifix and the blessed candles and the linen cloth
which is spread over the little table. Then I prepare a little jar with water and on a plate six pieces of clean white cotton wool with which the
different parts of the body will be wiped after anointing. Another
empty plate is put out on which the cotton wool will be placed
after use. I also show the children where the baptismal candles or
the blessed candles are kept which should be lit at the hour of death.
Then we tell them about our last wishes, which prayers we would
like to hear, which hymns to have sung, which garment we wish
to wear as our last. We discuss these matters once a year in our
family, and the horror that usually accompanies last sickness and
death diminishes greatly. With all the practical details settled in our
minds, there is greater calm and acceptance of the inevitable when
the final hours come. We also promise the children that we will
not delay to ask the priest, and make them promise to do the
same for us. After this yearly discussion, we take the texts of
the sacrament of Extreme Unction and read them through once. The
opening prayers are deeply soothing, addressed to the family rather
than to the sick themselves:

Let us pray. O Lord, Jesus Christ, let there enter this house with the entrance of our lowliness, eternal happiness, divine prosperity, serene gladness, fruitful charity, everlasting health; may there fly from this place all approach of the demons; let the angels of peace be present and all ill-feeling and discord leave this house. Make Thy Name great over us, O Lord, and bless our ministry, hallow the entrance of our lowliness, Thou Who art holy, Thou Who art kind and abideth with the Father and the Holy Ghost, world without end.

Let us pray and beseech Our Lord, Jesus Christ, that He would fill this dwelling with blessing and all that dwell therein and send them a good angel to be their guardian and make them His servants to study the wonders of His law; may He turn them from all contrary powers; may He save them from alarm and disturbance and vouchsafe to keep them in health in this dwelling Who, with the Father and the Holy Ghost, liveth and reigneth world without end. Amen.

Let us pray. Hear O Lord, Holy Father, Almighty and Eternal God, and vouchsafe to send Thy holy angel from heaven to watch over, to cherish, protect, visit and guard all them that dwell in this house, through Christ, Our Lord. Amen.

These first prayers haven't even touched on sickness and death yet. They pray for the peace and happiness of all who dwell in the house. Only then is the *Confiteor* said and then the priest turns to those present in the sick room and asks them to pray for the sick person during the administration of the sacrament. Then he says,

In the Name of the Father, and of the Son, and of the Holy Ghost. Let there be extinguished in thee all power of the devil by the imposition of our hands and by the invocation of all holy Angels, Archangels, Patriarchs, Prophets, Apostles, Martyrs, Confessors, Virgins and of all the Saints together. Amen.

After this the sacrament proper is administered—Holy Unction. The Fathers of the Church tell us that, by this Holy Unction, not only all sins of our whole life, even the ones we might have forgotten to mention in Confession, are forgiven, but also the remission of temporal punishment is obtained. Now the priest takes the holy oil and anoints the sick person on the closed eyes, the ears, the nose, the mouth, hands and feet, while he says, "By this holy unction and

His own most gracious mercy may the Lord forgive thee whatever
sin thou hast committed by sight, hearing, smell, taste, speech, touch.
Amen," repeating this holy formula each time as he touches the respective part of the person's body.

We never fail to read the most consoling prayer to be said after
death:

> Come to his assistance all ye Saints of God, meet him all ye Angels
> of God, receiving his soul, offering it in the sight of the Most High.
> May Christ receive thee Who has called thee and may the angels
> conduct thee to Abraham's bosom, receiving thy soul and offering
> it in the sight of the Most High.

This prayer is followed by the first recital of "Eternal rest give
unto him, O Lord, and let perpetual light shine upon him. Let
him rest in peace." Later, the Church, this true mother, turns to those
who are present, knowing that this is a heartrending moment for
them, and she prays:

> Grant, O God, that while we lament the departure of this, Thy
> servant, we may always remember that we are most certainly to
> follow him, and give us grace to prepare for that last hour by a good
> life, that we may not be surprised by a sudden and unprovided
> death, but be ever watching that, when Thou shalt call, we may
> with the Bridegroom enter into eternal glory, through Christ, Our
> Lord. Amen.

If death is approached in this spirit, we can only exclaim with
the Church at Easter: "O Death, where is thy victory? O Death,
where is thy sting?"

It is very important that we should make our family aware of the
festive character surrounding the administration of Holy Unction.
In a way it is a farewell gathering in honor of a beloved on the point
of leaving for a faraway country. We know we shall see him again,
but we do not know the hour, and we wish him Godspeed with
all our hearts.

Here we come to realize the true reason why the Church takes so
much pains to teach us how to celebrate, how to live life as one long,
uninterrupted solemn feast. She does this so that, on the crucial day,
we should be able to apply the wisdom gathered over a long time

and to celebrate as the greatest feast of all our departure for the heavenly Jerusalem. If we show our children in time the festive side of this great sacrament, we may be sure that, when the day comes, they will not kneel around our bed sobbing and crying, but all of us together will be able to answer the priest with a peaceful heart. "If you love me," we should say to our dear ones in the words of Our Lord, "you should rejoice with me because I am going to the Father." This is the spirit in which we should talk about death in our families.

In my life, rich in sickness and operations, I have received the sacrament of Holy Unction more than once. Each time I experienced the same profound peace—like homecoming after a stormy journey, and—each time I recovered! I am absolutely sure that these recoveries were due to a great extent to this very peace brought about by complete relaxation and abandonment to the will of God, which freed all mental energy for healing rather than wasting it in worry and anxiety.

And if one gets up from a sickbed after holy anointing—what a wonderful feeling! It is a new beginning. All sins were forgiven more thoroughly than ever in the sacrament of Penance; even the temporal punishment accumulated throughout one's life—that also is gone. Now, after having passed so closely by this last door, one appreciates more fully another chance to do better and to start with a clean slate.

THE CROSS

On the third of May the Church has us celebrate the feast of the Finding of the Cross. It is connected with the old tradition that the Empress Helena discovered the True Cross of Christ in the fourth century and built a church on that place. We may rest assured that this legend alone would not be reason enough for Holy Mother Church to install not only one but two feasts. For in September we celebrate the Exaltation of the Holy Cross. What the Church wants to bring home to us is this: that we must take the word of Our Lord seriously: "Whosoever wants to become my disciple, let him take up his cross and follow Me."

When we celebrate these feasts of the Cross in May and September in our family, this leads to talk about the different crosses in our life, small ones, big ones. When the children were little, we pointed out to them that having a slight headache or a running nose or an aching stomach is not a nuisance to be complained about. It is the form my daily cross takes today. Yesterday it might have been very bad weather when I was ready to go for a hike; or it might have been a most irritable and cranky mother who taxed the patience of the family. Tomorrow it might be. . . . And so we enumerate the different disguises under which the daily cross can show itself in our lives. Invariably we come to talk about the day when the cross would be a very heavy one, when one of our beloved ones—mother, father, sister, or brother—would be taken away from us. In this manner, also, we prepare our minds in advance for these happenings, and again we stress to the children that the day of our death on earth should be regarded as our true birthday, our birthday in heaven, which we should never begrudge to anyone we love. We should think of our dead as of ones who have won the battle and have gone to their eternal reward, out of reach of harm. Even if we could do so, we should not wish them back.

FAMILY RETREATS

If it is at all possible—and it's amazing how many things are possible where there is a will—families should try to take a few days off together every year for a family retreat. If we have to stand the heat of noonday together, we should also be together when we ask and receive help.

Though absolute silence is generally recommended during retreats, we have found them the right time to talk with our children on subjects that concern them deeply and intimately. For instance, on the mysteries of childbirth. Why should we wait for strangers—doctors or teachers—to give our children sex talks in school when this touches on the most sacred precincts in our life? The way in which such knowledge comes to a child can make it or break it, and as no one can know a child as intimately as the parents do, we should guard this instruction as our most indisputable right.

Another important topic with our adolescent children were the threefold vocations—to the married life, to the priesthood, to the unmarried life in the world. We tried to make them aware that one of the three is the state in which God wants them to spend their life and that it was up to them and their untiring prayer to find out the right one. If God wanted them in the unmarried state, this, we pointed out to them, had to be a sacrifice brought knowingly, voluntarily, willingly. If, however, they found that God called them to the married state, we did all in our power to keep them from taking this lightly. The contemporary craze for "going steady" when young people are much too young to make such weighty decisions, having blind dates, etc., is unwholesome and dangerous. With the Hollywood version of love set up on all sides before them, we tried to make them realize the true nature of love—a love that is stronger than death. And as it is sometimes easier to make one's point by a concrete example, we would show them a fruit picked fresh from the tree, a plum or a peach with that light fuzz on it as a sign that it had not been handled. Then we would pass such a fruit around the table, each one holding it for a time. When it came back to the first person, it was still a perfectly good plum—not worm-eaten, nothing wrong with it, and still—it didn't look appetizing. It lacked the bloom of freshness. It was too much handled. Girls and boys who change their partners frequently, talking love and acting it in kisses and hugs—well, there isn't very much wrong with that, anybody might say, but still it is as with the plum: such a girl, such a boy, has lost this indescribable freshness; he or she no longer comes untouched from the hands of God. Young people readily understand what we mean by that.

ENGAGEMENT AND WEDDING

We felt that such talks were indispensable, that we owed them to our children, especially in a time when sex assails them through advertisements, in magazines, newspapers, television, radio—wherever they turn. They have to get the right bearing, and where should they get it if not from their parents? They have to be fortified, in order to be able, when the time comes, to choose a partner *for life.* If they have been brought up from their earliest years to do nothing, however insignificant, without first considering whether it conformed with the will of God—and this is something only to be found out in prayer—when they reach their twenties they will most certainly apply this most important lesson for this most important decision. Is he—is she—the one with whom I can become a saint more quickly than alone? This was the final test adopted in our family. (It leaves out of consideration, as points of much less importance, such questions as: "What is his job?" "How much is he earning?" "What does he look like?" "Is she pretty?" "Is she musical?" etc., etc.) When this one question has been answered with "Yes," our young people decide to get engaged before the Church. In the old country it is the custom that the boy and girl give each other engagement rings. These rings are blessed by the priest, not as solemnly as the wedding ring, but the blessing turns them from ordinary rings into a sacramental. While they put these rings on each other's finger, they pronounce solemnly their intention to marry and this solemn promise binds them before God and men. Of course, this is a family feast and a day of great rejoicing for everybody. The two young people sit in the place of honor and are showered with presents from the family. These are the gifts they get before the invitations are sent out and wedding presents start to arrive from the outside.

As every member of every family is an individual, unlike anybody else, the ways of celebrating such an engagement were different with each child. Some of our children wanted a very quiet celebration, and "no guests, please." Others, however, wanted a hilarious evening after the solemnity in church, with folk dancing and punch and games and lots of fun. That is why one can never rely on a handbook treating how to celebrate feasts. So much depends on the individuality of the people who do the celebrating.

The days between engagement and wedding are dedicated to preparations—but not, first and foremost, as the world seems to emphasize in all the magazines "for the bride," on the preparation of the material goods alone—furniture, household utensils, dresses, dresses, and more dresses. Our first concern is with laying a solid foundation for the couple's new life. For this, we set aside a first preparation period right after the engagement, and an immediate preparation during the last days before the wedding. During the first preparation period, we have the young couple discuss with the parents (as a rule the parents of the bride) all the important facets of family life. This we do on the evenings of a full week. The discussions include, of course, the prayer life of a family—morning prayer, grace before and after meals, evening prayer; a resolution to say the rosary together at least at certain times of the year (such as during May, the month of Mary; during October, the month of the rosary; during November, for the souls of the departed; on all the eves of a feast of Mary). We speak about preparation for Mass before Sundays and great feast days; about pilgrimages—all such devotions being family devotions. And we tell the young people that later, when children arrive, they should be associated with the prayer life of the family as soon as possible, even if they do not yet understand what it is all about. The young soul will always respond to the atmosphere of prayer.

Another topic on these evenings is the daily cross, which will never be found wanting—how to prepare for it, how to meet it, how to learn to carry it ungrudgingly and willingly, and as long as possible with a smile. Such an attitude, we tell them, will keep a marriage from getting "on the rocks."

And of course we talk about love—what its true nature is, and what it is not. The thirteenth chapter of the First Epistle of St. Paul to the Corinthians is as good a guide in this respect as any.

Then there is the imitation of Christ in the life of a family. "I have given you an example and I want you to do as I have done" is an excellent motto for a young family. To keep one's eye on the Lord, to get used to the idea of saying, "What would He do now? What would He say in my place?" provides the most reliable method for bringing up children.

Evidently each of the young, boy and girl, have their special problems and questions, and their own ideas to discuss; and the family into which he or she marries will each have their own views to bring out. The essential thing for us, however, was and is that there should be a full week set aside for such a first preparation for married life, as a meeting not only of the hearts but also of the minds.

Then comes the time when the young bride prepares her bridal gown. In our family this important garment is prepared at home, with the help of the mother and sisters. This may sound very old-fashioned, but the hours spent in loving work together seem to us very precious, and many loving thoughts and resolutions are stitched into the bridal gown.

The weeks pass, perhaps the months, and the time for the wedding itself approaches. The first few days of the week preceding the wedding we reserve for the last and most important talks. Throughout their young lives the young people have received all the information on sex necessary to the stages in their development. Strangely enough these seem to come in cycles of seven: when the child is seven years old it is ready for its first story about God sending the child and letting it grow under the mother's heart for nine months, until she gives it life with great pain. This first talk creates a firm bond between mother and child. About seven years later the child is on the threshold of puberty and needs more enlightenment and instruction. Now it has to face the realities of sex, and learn how to deal with its problems. This instruction should be frank, clear, and explicit. We cannot afford to leave our children in ignorance in times such as ours. This information need not be given in one discussion only. We have always given our children the opportunity of asking questions as they came to their minds.

But during the last days before the wedding, a new kind of approach seems to be called for. Now is the moment to speak of the union of husband and wife as a fulfillment, as a source of joy. Too many of our manuals are one-sided in their discussion of sex. We should tell our children of the true value and the God-givenness of healthy and sound sex life—though not for its own sake. We should try to make them see it as a symbol of the greatest thing in creation: as our soul longs to be one with God, as all our striving for perfection is toward that one end—our union with God—we have a perfect symbol for this fusion in the most intimate union of husband and wife. In this light only does sex life find its true evaluation and place.

I have always deplored the fact that there is a tendency among certain writers and theologians to put a stigma on the married state in its relation to holiness. These people seem to regret that certain saints were married; if they could hush it up, they no doubt would. But there is no getting around it: there was a St. Catherine of Genoa, a St. Monica and a St. Elizabeth of Hungary, a great St. Louis of France, and the excellent family man, St. Thomas More, to mention only a few among many, many others. I feel that the Church has placed these great heroic figures in the forefront of the canonized saints in order to assure us that sanctity is not incompatible with married life. And how absurd such a thought would be! Only if we see marriage as a great sacrament, the symbol of the relationship between Christ and the Church, between the soul and God during all eternity, only then chastity becomes meaningful as a *sacrifice,* when marriage is given up voluntarily by our priests and religious. What good would it be to offer up something second-rate, something we shouldn't want anyhow? Again, how absurd!

These thoughts belong to our final preparation during the first three days of the last week. The second three days the young couple retire and make a retreat, either under the direction of a priest-friend, or, if this is not possible, by themselves, their discussions on the spiritual life in the family having provided them with ample food for prayer and meditation.

In our family, we keep alive an age-old custom, that of telling of the "Tobias Nights." Father or mother advise the bride and bride-groom-to-be to read now the book of Tobias. There, in the sixth chapter, the Archangel Raphael, guardian and friend of young Tobias, admonishes the young man: "They who in such manner receive matrimony, as to shut out God from themselves, and from their mind, and to give themselves to their lust, as the horse and mule, which have no understanding, over them the devil has power. But thou when thou shalt take her, go into chamber and for three days keep thyself continent from her, and give thyself to nothing else but prayers with her." From this passage derives an old custom that young married couples spend the first three nights in prayer and meditation together before they start their married life. This may sound rather startling advice nowadays, but some of my married children returning from their honeymoon, quite freely spoke about the release from tension and apprehension it had provided to them. But it should by no means be taken as a general rule, it is a question of personality.

On the day before the wedding feast our young people return from their retreat, strengthened in mind and spirit, and ready for the great day.

The evening before the wedding is celebrated, as in the old country, as the *Polterabend*, again a survival from pagan times when the people with great noise and much singing, chanting, and music wanted to shy away the evil spirits. The Church has taken over and Christianized this folk custom. All our guests are invited to come the day before the feast—and the feast day receives its vigil. There is a festive dinner with the two young people sitting for the last time each with their parents. Afterwards, the evening is spent in merry-making, folk dancing, games, and music. Around ten o'clock, however, the feast is over and ends with family evening prayers. Of course, this again varies according to the wishes of the bride. Once we had only nine guests present, and the last time, at my youngest daughter Lorli's wedding, we were about a hundred and forty.

The next morning finds mother and daughter for the last time in their intimate closeness. Now I assist the bride to put on her bridal gown and to fasten the veil to her hair. Then she kneels down while the bridal wreath made of fresh white flowers is placed over the veil, at which time the solemn words are said: "Receive here this symbol of your virginity which I have helped you to keep intact that you may give it unspotted to your husband as your greatest gift," to which the daughter answers with a heartfelt, "Thank you. Praised be God." This is always a moment of deep emotion. After the last long embrace I sign the forehead of my daughter with the sign of the Cross and then lead her downstairs, where the procession is already formed.

In Tyrolia, that part of Austria where I come from, the parish priest leads the bride to the altar. They are the last couple in the procession, which is headed by the bridegroom leading the bride's mother. And that's the way we do it in our family. And so we attend the Nuptial Mass and listen, deeply moved, to the words of the priest:

Dear friends in Christ: As you know, you are about to enter into a union which is most sacred and most serious, a union which was established by God Himself. By it He gave to man a share in the greatest work of creation, the work of the continuation of the human race. And in this way He sanctified human love and enabled man and woman to help each other live as children of God, by sharing a common life under His fatherly care.

Because God Himself is thus its author, marriage is of its very nature a holy institution, requiring of those who enter into it a complete and unreserved giving of self. But Christ Our Lord added to the holiness of marriage an even deeper meaning and a higher beauty. He referred to the love of marriage to describe His own love for His Church, that is, for the people of God whom He redeemed by His own blood. And so He gave to Christians a new vision of what married life ought to be, a life of self-sacrificing love like His own. It is for this reason that His Apostle, St. Paul, clearly states that marriage is now and for all time to be considered a great mystery, intimately bound up with the supernatural union of Christ and the Church, which union is also to be its pattern.

This union is most serious, because it will bind you together for life in a relationship so close and so intimate, that it will profoundly influence your whole future. That future, with its hopes and disappointments, its successes and its failures, its pleasures and its pains, its joys and its sorrows, is hidden from your eyes. You know that these elements are mingled in every life, and are to be expected in your own. And so, not knowing what is before you, you take each other for better or for worse, for richer or for poorer, in sickness and in health, until death.

Truly, then, these words are most serious. It is a beautiful tribute to your undoubted faith in each other, that, recognizing their full import, you are nevertheless so willing and ready to pronounce them. And because these words involve such solemn obligations, it is most fitting that you rest the security of your wedded life upon the great principle of self-sacrifice. And so you begin your married life by the voluntary and complete surrender of your individual lives in the interest of that deeper and wider life which you are to have in common. Henceforth you belong entirely to each other, you will be one in mind, one in heart, and one in affections. And whatever sacrifices you may hereafter be required to make to preserve this common life, always make them generously. Sacrifice is usually difficult and irksome. Only love can make it easy; and perfect love can make it a joy. We are willing to give in proportion as we love. And when love is perfect, the sacrifice is complete. God so loved the world that He gave His only begotten Son, and the Son so loved us that He gave Himself for our salvation. "Greater love than this no man hath, that a man lay down his life for his friends."

No greater blessing can come to your married life than pure conjugal love, loyal and true to the end. May, then, this love with which you join your hands and hearts today, never fail, but grow deeper and stronger as the years go on. And if true love and the unselfish spirit of perfect sacrifice guide your every action, you can expect the greatest measure of earthly happiness that may be allotted to man in this vale of tears. The rest is in the hands of God. Nor will God be wanting to your needs; He will pledge you the life-long support of His graces in the holy sacrament which you are now going to receive.

And then we all receive Holy Communion with the new husband and the new wife. After this ceremony, all friends present can congratulate and wish God's blessing and happiness with confidence knowing that the fulfillment of their wish has already begun.

We see to it that the table is most beautifully decorated—if possible it should be a sitting-down meal. This is the time for speeches. The father of the bride will address his daughter and the father of the bridegroom will address his son. Somebody will thank the friends and the guests for sharing this great day with the family.

When the meal is over and guests and friends are still standing around, the young couple disappear quietly. Hand in hand they go over to the house altar; while the young bride bows her head her husband takes the white wreath from her. Together they place it a

he feet of the Blessed Mother and make the sign of the cross on each
ther's forehead. It is the first act in their new life.

A little later everyone will wave good-bye as they get into the car
o start their journey through life together.

This is one of the beauties of a large family: when the older ones
eave the house to marry, the younger ones take their places, and
when the youngest is still in grade school, grandchildren are already
arriving for long visits around Christmas, Easter, and summer va-
cation. There are always children around—the next living links in
the chain of the generations—learning from their elders the most
important lesson of all: how to celebrate the feasts of their life.